Perspectives on a Parent Movement

The Revolt of Parents of Children with Intellectual Limitations

Rosemary F. Dybwad

BROOKLINE
BOOKS

Library of Congress Cataloging-in-Publication Data

Dybwad, Rosemary Ferguson, 1910-
    Perspective on a parent movement: the revolt of parents of
children with intellectual limitation/ by Rosemary Ferguson Dybwad.
      p.   cm.
    Includes bibliographical references.
    ISBN 0-914797-74-3
    1. Mentally handicapped children. 2. Parents of handicapped
children. 3. Mentally handicapped children--Legal status, laws,
etc. I. Title.
HV891.D96   1990
362.3'083--dc20   90-35065
                                                 CIP

Contents

PART V: Employment and Rehabilitation

PART VI: Human Rights

PART VII: The Image and The Reality

PART VIII: Religious Concerns

Preface

Rosemary Dybwad has enriched the lives of all who have met her. But she has also influenced the lives of literally millions of people who will never hear her name.

This book celebrates her life and work over a period of 80 years not only by bringing together many of her papers and talks but also by illustrating the fundamentally human concerns which inspire her. Throughout her life, she has always succeeded in integrating a truly international vision of human potential with a day to day interest in the lives of ordinary people - above all, people with mental handicap about whom many fine speeches are made but who are rarely consulted themselves. She was among the very first to insist they were people first, human beings with needs and rights, fellow citizens rather than objects of charity or compassion. She moves just as easily among them as she does among professionals, politicians and world leaders.

Equally important in her life are parents and family members all over the world. She was involved in the earliest beginnings of the spontaneous movement of parents joining together, whether for mutual support, for advocacy, for innovative ideas or for bringing home to governments and to the general public the needs and rights of people with mental handicap.

She and Gunnar Dybwad must hold the world record in accumulating flying miles on behalf of people with mental handicap — so much so that the world's airlines ought to donate them a permanent free travel pass. There are few countries which she has not visited and virtually no country about which she cannot provide helpful information and useful contact points — not just the official bodies but the address of a particular family or individual, all helped by her legendary prodigious memory. These visits brought her into direct contact with parents all over the world and led directly to the establishment of innumerable voluntary organizations in many countries and localities.

As if all this were not enough, she has just produced the 3rd edition of the *International Directory of Mental Retardation Resources*. Following the earlier editions of 1971 and 1979, the 1989 version reflects radical changes in the field of mental handicap. More governments now officially recognize their responsibilities; many more voluntary organizations have been established at local and national levels, 124 of whom in 78 countries are members of the International League of Societies for Persons with Mental Handicap. The 1989 edition not only documents the work of its tireless editor and the developments which she helped to inspire, it also records the radical changes which are still needed to bring people with mental handicap fully into the mainstream of society.

This collection of speeches and talks given all over the world richly convey both her essential modesty and her passionate commitment to progress. They provide a challenging agenda for the 1990's and for the 21st century.

PETER MITTLER

Professor of Special Education, University of
*   Manchester, England*
Immediate Past President, International League of
*   Societies for persons with Mental Handicap*

Introduction

by Robert Perske

Now comes this precious book of speeches by Rosemary Dybwad—
a book destined to be one more of her international treasures.
Without her knowledge, it has been carefully and lovingly put
together by her husband and her colleagues. The value of this
book, however, will become vividly apparent as soon as the reader
considers *when* she said what she did.

The young have a cocky way of thinking that history begins
with them. It was meant to be, I suppose. Otherwise, our world
might never utilize its new life and fresh innovations and move
forward. But maybe—just maybe—the young leaders in the field
of mental handicap, who now hold their own new programs so
high, will be interested in knowing how Rosemary had helped to
plant seeds in our thinking many years ago-seeds that gave rise to
much of the best we are doing for people with mental handicap
today:

- Today, everyone talks about parent-to-parent efforts, parent-
  driven programs and parent-professional partnerships. You
  will find that Rosemary and her close colleagues dreamed
  about such parent power—even citing isolated examples from
  across the world in an age when most professionals believed
  that parents would be too traumatized to be of any substantial
  help to their own sons and daughters with mental handicap.

- Self-advocacy organizations (people with mental handicap
  helping one another to speak for themselves) are beginning to
  spring up all over the world. And yet Rosemary described a
  small group of people helping one another in Stockholm in the
  early 1960's—an interesting little effort inspired by Bengt Nirje.

- Supported employment and job coaching programs have come alive in many countries. And yet, twenty years ago, Rosemary described a "Pathway Scheme" being utilized by factories in Wales that possessed some of the functions being perfected in such programs today.

- Rosemary and her colleagues spoke valiantly against the centuries-long habit of viewing people with mental handicap as "children forever." And, although the term *transitioning into adulthood* had yet to be coined, much of what she predicted has influenced the full-citizen programs being developed today.

- In the early days when people with all kinds of backgrounds joined together and scrapped for ways people with mental handicap could be helped, she called for a day when countries would possess many-faceted arrays of voluntary and professional organizations doing different functions. That day is arriving now in many countries.

- In an age when service deliverers did almost nothing for children until they were of school age, she described any early childhood program she could find and she wondered "why does early intervention have to come so late?" Today, in many countries, young workers have created beautiful answers to this question that used to pain her so much.

- Today, a new wave of educators work vigorously on inclusion programs-carefully placing students with mental handicap in regular school classrooms, building circles of friends around them. In Rosemary's speeches, you will find her amplifying statements by Jack Tizard of England, predicting a time when regular educators would become substantially involved in the education of those with mental handicap.

And so, the reader of this book has an opportunity to discover hundreds of seeds like these in her speeches. And you—young parent, leading edge professional or recently-attracted volunteer citizen—don't be too quick to pass off the attitudes and programs she described by saying, "Oh yes, we already have that." *Consider the date when she talked about it.* Then you will sense the forward thinking of this woman and grasp the true value of this book.

By the time this book comes off the presses, Rosemary will have passed her 80th birthday. To which many of us will say, "So what?" While many other people have already given up their forging ahead and have retired to their gardens and their memories, Rosemary and Gunnar refuse to do it. They continue to interact emotionally and professionally with people on the leading edge-and their own output continues to be ten times the sum of two persons at work. They continue to travel the world, observing and sharing ideas as they go. Their words continue to grab readers as if they had been written or spoken by twenty-year-olds.

When Rosemary Ferguson of Howe, Indiana and Gunnar Dybwad of Leipzig, Germany planned their 1934 marriage, their differences had to be obvious. Some observers must have rolled their eyes and said, "Nothing good will come of this marriage."

They got married anyway—and all of us are better for it.

Fortunately Rosemary and Gunnar never got stuck on merely beholding each other like many couples do (although we've often caught them gazing fondly at each other). They began looking together in the same direction—focusing intensely on whatever it was that diminished and hurt and stomped on the dreams of people with mental handicap and their families.

And so, for 56 years, dignity-and justice-hungry Gunnar—with an array of passions and a nose for breakthroughs—has moved over the earth leaping and landing on every action and attitude that can make life better for people with mental handicap and their families. And for 56 years, quiet, strong, archivist-par-excellence, Rosemary has traveled with him as a lovely stabilizing fulcrum. Together, they have helped us all to leverage a revolution on behalf of persons with mental handicap that would have been unthinkable just four decades ago.

Although Gunnar's leading edge opinions have influenced us all, we often learned to know and care about people in Nairobi,

Beirut, Canberra, Tokyo, Peshawar, Auckland, Vancouver, Uppsala and hundreds of other faraway places—by hearing about them from Rosemary and seeing them through her eyes.

Rosemary became our unofficial international network leader in the 1950's, when Gunnar served as Executive Director of what is now known as the Association for Retarded Citizens in the United States—when its small offices were just a few steps away from New York City's Grand Central Station and a short ride from two of the largest international airports in the world. Rosemary graciously welcomed travelers into that office, invited them to share their experiences, and she produced the first international newsletter.

When Gunnar became Director of the Mental Retardation Project for the International Union for Child Welfare in Geneva Switzerland (1964-67), Rosemary occupied an adjacent office and continued her networking mission as she has done throughout her career. Then both were invited to work side by side at Brandeis University's Heller School for Advanced Studies in Social Work. Again they could be found in adjacent offices working long hours alone and in unison and going home together each evening.

Believe it or not, Gunnar's office was tidy! Not so with Rosemary's. Journalist Steve McFadden, in a 1978 feature article in *Boston Today* described her work place:

> Her office is a quagmire of data. The chairs are smothered in studies, and the walls fairly groan from the accumulated weight of a total bookcase environment. She sits before burly heaps of printed matter, literally walled in by towering stacks of information from around the world. She labors placidly, her blue eyes taciturn pools of understanding as she imperturbably scans yet another document.

And what has all this glorious cutter helped to produce?

- During her career, the International League of Societies for Persons with Mental Handicap (ILSMH) was born, an organization that today has connected kindred-spirted organizations from over 80 countries.

- She served as the inspiration for the Rosemary F. Dybwad International Awards, a program begun in 1963 by the Association for Retarded Citizens (US), that has enabled better than 60 awardees to travel, study and write about mental handicap in other countries. I was one of those lucky recipients, took time off from my job in an institution in Kansas, in 1969, and traveled throughout Sweden and Denmark, studying fresh attitudes, trailblazing laws and innovative programs for people with mental handicap. The ideas gleaned from those travels continue to serve as springboards for my thinking today. It helped me gain a number of international colleagues with whom I continue lively interactions to this day. And it connected me with one of the warmest, most-knowledgeable, always-on-call mentors one could ever have in Rosemary. Multiply such a happening by 60 and one can see how the Dybwad Award Program has become one of the least expensive, most efficient global information sharing experiences of the century.

- Three editions of the *International Directory of Mental Retardation Resources* have been produced that list key agencies and publications in many countries throughout the world. Each directory had been compiled and edited in her office, the latest coming off the presses in 1989.

A year and a half ago, Rosemary was invited to give the final speech at a four-state self-advocacy conference in Stamford, Connecticut. She arrived on the opening day. For two days she attended all sessions, listened to everything and took many notes. Then on the last hour of the last day, Rosemary Dybwad responded to them like a loving, reigning queen would do it. In simple words, she reflected all the rich things she had observed. She described things self-advocates had been doing in other countries.

The self-advocates and their helpers became wide-eyed and quiet as they listened to her soft, sincere voice. They understood every word she said. They listened as if they had been slaves about

to receive freedom papers. And they loved her for what she said.
   There was a day when many of the speeches in this book did
exactly that for other audiences.

April 16, 1990

REFERENCES

Dybwad, Rosemary. ed. (1989). *International Directory of Mental Retardation Resources Third Edition*. Washington, DC: President's Committee on Mental Retardation; Brussels: International Societies for Persons with Mental Handicap.

McFadden, Steve (1978). Coupled for a Common Flight. *Boston Today*. date.

Perske, Robert, ed. (1987). *How We Shared Life Experiences-The Second Inter-State Seminar on Self Advocacy (Connecticut. New Jersey. New York and Pennsylvania)*. New York, United Nations Plaza: InterServ.

Editor's Note

This collection of Rosemary Dybwad's speeches was prepared for her 80th birthday without her knowledge and participation. Some of these speeches go back two decades and more and contain language no longer acceptable today. These terms are certainly no longer used by Dr. Dybwad. However it was decided not to edit the papers for terminology because that would have interfered with the historical content of these presentations.

PART I

The Widening Role of Parent Organizations Around the World

Chapter 1

Mental Handicap: The World Scene*

The International League of Societies for the Mentally Handicapped, founded in 1969, brings together parent sponsored associations from all over the world. In Britain, France, Yugoslavia, and Denmark, in New Zealand and Australia, in Japan, India, Hong Kong, and Indonesia, in Ghana and Kenya, Poland and Spain, across Latin America and on the Caribbean Islands, there exist parent associations, functioning on every level of the "developmental continuum."

The League in 1975 has some 85 member societies in 60 different countries, and every year more are being added.

Concerned parents in India or in Brazil, in New Zealand, Lebanon, Mauritius, or Belgium are, of course, primarily motivated by the desire and the duty to get help for their handicapped children. Yet they soon learn that the help the child needs must come from services—educational services, vocational services, residential services, guardianship services—and to secure them, the parents must band together with the other parents, must keep the pressure on public officials and legislators, and must enlist the aid of professional workers and civic organizations.

It is this basic similarity of their needs and concerns that has provided the strong impetus for the parent organizations and has made them, throughout the world, among the most visible and potent consumer groups in the field of human services. And it is this that underlies one of the International League's major functions, the exchange of information.

---

* Kings Fund Centre , London, 1975

There is no one country which has all the answers for coping with the problem of mental retardation. New discoveries are made, new developments take place in many countries, and one of the main functions of the parent associations has been to act as an international communications network to make new developments more widely known and to insist—and insist—that the authorities put this new knowledge to use.

Here, may I say, lies the difference between the International League and its professional counterpart, the International Association for the Scientific Study of Mental Deficiency, officially established in 1964. In its congresses, which meet every three years, the IASSMD provides a forum where researchers and persons from the many disciplines involved in providing services present new findings, critiques of previously formulated theories, and evaluations of existing services. But the IASSMD as such does not formulate policies, does not propose new services. It provides a presumably neutral ground for professional interchange.

The International League, on the other hand, is an action oriented organization, and the most notable of its many policy statements is the Rights Declaration it promulgated in 1968, which subsequently, in 1971, was adopted by the General Assembly of the United Nations, and is, without doubt, the single most important and influential document in the field of mental retardation.

Let me give you one example of an area where action initiated by the parent sponsored association has led in many countries even to a change of its own name, such as the change in the USA from National Association for Retarded *Children* to National Association for Retarded *Citizens*. That mentally retarded children grow up to become mentally retarded adults might not strike you as an example of new knowledge, yet if one takes a look at the way programs are developed and implemented it becomes very obvious how few services there are available for the adults, how little recognition there is of what mentally retarded adult persons need and what they can contribute, and anyone who takes a realistic look at programs for retarded children will see how far we still have to go in preparing them for adult living.

Traditionally, we have seen the answer to the needs of the

mentally retarded essentially in medical and educational programs; indeed, for many of the mentally retarded even the need for
educational programs was denied. However, when we look at the
many years they will spend out of school as compared with the
years they spend in school, then we recognize strikingly different
and important program needs for which as yet we have made too
little provision.

Measures need to be taken to provide the necessities of life for
these handicapped adults—in particular, financial assistance,
opportunities for meaningful occupation, and other aspects of
adult living such as health care, social activities, and spiritual life.
There is an urgent need to recognize that mental handicap is
rapidly becoming a major program area in social service, calling
for action from that sector of our public life. All of this adds up to
a multitude of legislative proposals, organizational changes in
public services, different patterns of staffing, and new budgetary
requirements, for which both initiative and support had to come
from the parent sponsored associations. It also involved the
seeking of new alliances with practitioners in disciplines previously not concerned with mental handicap, and the sometimes
traumatic and not infrequently controversial lessening of dependence on professional groups that had assumed an all-too-paternal-
istic, domineering role in the field.

Thus the movement initiated and carried by the associations
for the mentally handicapped is in ferment almost everywhere.
There are striking similarities in their patterns of organization and
development, but also some acute disagreements as to the future
role and function of the associations, the kind of membership they
should attract, the way in which they should seek financial support, and the specific programs they should pursue.

A clearer perspective can be achieved from a view of the
historical developments of the movement, using the last three
decades as a frame of reference. The 1940s saw the beginnings of
parent groups, most of them either fairly closely tied to a particular
service such as a residential institution, or else themselves managing a self-help project, a day school, or a recreation program. Fairly
soon the need was recognized for a broader base, for the develop-

ment of a national concern and national action.

Thus the decade of the 1950s saw the development of national organizations which derived their strength from a network of local and regional state member associations. The emphasis at first was still largely on cooperative self-help action but was increasingly broadened to include demands for governmental assistance and the recognition of the need to work with experts from various professions. Primary emphasis still focused on providing direct services for retarded *children*.

The third decade, the 1960s, might be called the decade of sophistication. It brought a more realistic recognition of the immensity of the problem of mental retardation, both in terms of the numbers affected and the multiplicity of services required during one retarded person's entire lifetime. The need for broad, multi-faceted governmental action was recognized, and in many countries the associations called for and aimed at participation in government commissions to study the needs and coordinate more effectively services for the mentally retarded.

While there had been some international communication in the form of personal visits and correspondence between leaders of the movement in various countries from the early beginnings, the 1960s saw the realization and recognition of a formal international organization, the International League of Societies for the Mentally Handicapped.

The 1970s seem to have led to a period of organizational introspection. As Dr. Sterner of Sweden expressed it recently, the associations are asking themselves, "Who are we and what do we want to be?"

Earlier this year my husband and I had the opportunity of serving as consultants in assisting a task force of the Canadian Association for the Mentally Retarded to review its purpose, function, and organizational structure. While the Canadian Association may, in certain areas, be farther advanced than those in some European countries, Dr. Sterner's survey confirmed that the following excerpt from the (unpublished) Canadian task force report represents the trend toward which the longer established organizations are moving.

Associations for the Mentally Retarded, like any other social institution, are operating in a world which is changing for mentally handicapped people just as it is changing for all of us. Such associations have to take account of current trends which are bound to affect the way they go about their primary aim. These trends suggest that the associations can best meet this challenge by:

a)   assuring the handicapped individual services in his own local area

b)   assuring him services which will tend to integrate rather than segregate him from the ordinary patterns of life in that area

c)   emphasizing and strengthening the most important social context of the individual: families with a handicapped child are seen now as units to be cherished and supported rather than units which have to be broken up by a recommendation for early residential care.

At the same time [that] government is increasingly involved in direct provision and operation of services, mental retardation is increasingly seen in conjunction with other disabilities, such as the so-called developmental disabilities (Cerebral Palsy, Epilepsy, and other disorders), and, more broadly, all social services are increasingly seen as part of a whole which is categorized by individual need rather than administrative label: i.e., the generic approach to planning and provision.

If the associations are to continue to be as effective in the future in achieving their first aim—the fulfillment of the individual handicapped person—as they have been in the past, they clearly have to take account of these trends. This in turn will mean finding new and exciting roles, new answers to some of the organizational questions which the current heart-searching is all about.

The changing trends in the field of mental retardation which are producing net challenges for Associations for the Mentally Retarded can be identified as follows:

1.   **From service provision to demonstrating new ideas**
This does not mean that the associations will stop providing services. Far from it. It means, though, that instead of providing basic services they will be constantly looking to ways to fill gaps and add dimensions to the lives of handicapped people. It is hard to see a time when this vital role will be over in a society which is constantly changing at a rate with which statutory provision simply cannot keep up.

2. **From service provision to demonstrating new ideas**
   This does not mean that the associations will manage the services provided by the state. Management and advisory committees cannot act as monitors; they can only act as managers and advisors, BUT we are living at a time when the need for truly independent monitors is well acknowledged. They are not tied by management considerations or the need to reconcile conflicting professional views; they can go STRAIGHT for the good of the individual person. This is a tremendously exciting new opportunity for voluntary associations in the field of mental retardation.

3. **From a narrow concern for mentally regarded people to a wider concern with all handicapped people**
   This does not mean that the interests of mentally retarded people will be swamped. Far from it. It means that the "lobbying" strength of the associations concerned with them will be able to unite with other groups and so grow, while at the same time protecting the special interests of retarded people. By extension, the associations will be able, through their own special interest, to spearhead some critical looks at the way our societies are going and what they offer to their weaker citizens. A good example here is the associations' proper concern with prevention of mental retardation. We know that the most important field of prevention lies in tackling the inner city problems of poverty and deprivation; work here by the associations is bound to have long lasting and far reaching effects on the health of society as a whole.

4. **From an organization primarily for parents to an organization for and with mentally handicapped people themselves**
   Handicapped people have, in the past, been largely left out of the decisions which can affect their lives quite vitally. The associations, in their recognition of the need to give handicapped people a voice, are already starting to lead the way in the sort of "consumer involvement" which will be the basis for the better services of the future. At the same time, it is the associations, through their special interest and expertise, who can do like none else the vital job of introducing the handicapped person to his "normal" peers and so ensure that his integration into society is a real one and not just a paper one.

5. **From an organization which does what others can do to an organization which provides what no one else can**
   This does not mean that the traditional involvement and hard work

of parents which has developed the associations until now will be forgotten in future. Quite the contrary. Parents, members, freed from the heavy responsibilities for providing services, will be able to concentrate on the one area which no professional, no other person, can do as well: the counseling of parents who have just met their own retarded child. The "pilot parent" projects are the beginning of a new strength for parent members.

In summary, the associations find themselves now at a tremendously exciting time of change. They will have an increasing freedom from the many heavy responsibilities of the past which will enable them to launch new creative efforts for the decades to come. They will be relieved from the responsibilities of things which other people can do to turn to things which they can do better than anyone else.

I hope that this brief excerpt from the Canadian report has given you an appreciation of the important continuing role that awaits the active and progressive associations of parents and friends of mentally handicapped citizens. Let me now call your attention to another development, a closer working together but also from time to time a closer confrontation between these national associations and national governments.

Denmark was the first country to prescribe, by statute, representation from the Association of Parents of the Mentally Retarded, both on the national and the regional mental retardation boards. For many years this 1959 Danish legislation remained unique, but in more recent years some other countries have introduced similar arrangements. Switzerland has established a standing commission on retardation, an advisory body, after long effort by the Swiss Federation of Parents of the Mentally Handicapped, and its president serves as chairman. Persistent work by the Norwegian association resulted last year in a national regulation establishing in each county a three-member "watch-dog" committee to monitor adequacy of retardation services. A representative of the county's parent association serves on the committee.

In some other countries, such as Belgium, Sweden, Spain, and Australia, there are government appointed national commissions dealing with all handicaps on which the associations for the mentally retarded are represented. It is noteworthy that in Spain this commission works within the Department of Labor, Spain having been one of the first countries to recognize that sheltered workshops and vocational training centers must of necessity be considered in the context of labor policy.

In France, UNAPEI, the national parents' association, issues a comprehensive monthly bulletin which reports on and reviews in great detail proposed new legislation, regulations, and governmental activities in the field of retardation and related disabilities.

Switzerland was the first country to develop a national policy for subsidies to local associations for the mentally handicapped, on the condition that they were providing information and counseling services to parents. The significant point is that it was the Swiss governmental disability insurance system which provided this financial subsidy because they had convinced themselves that these kinds of services, rendered by local parent association, were of distinct value as measures in secondary prevention of disability.

It has been a characteristic of any of the older and larger parent associations to develop an interest in international exchange and to become part of the international network of helping organizations. A look at this network seems appropriate at this point.

A resolution passed in 1950 by the United Nations General Assembly, which led to the establishment of the rehabilitation program within the United Nations, requested the Secretary General to plan this activity jointly with the UN Specialized Agencies and in consultation with the interested non-governmental organizations. A meeting of such organizations was called and resulted in 1953 in the formation of the Council of World Organizations Interested in the Handicapped, also known as CWOIH. CWOIH now comprises almost 40 international voluntary organizations, from the International Committee of the Red Cross to the World Federation of the Deaf and the World Council for the Blind, from the International Catholic Child Bureau to the Salvation Army. A major force from the beginning was the International Society for Rehabilitation of the Disabled, now also called Rehabilitation International. Its Secretary General, Mr. Norman Acton, is at present the chairman of CWOIH, and the International League of Societies for the Mentally Handicapped is represented on its

Executive. One of the most recent members is the International Cerebral Palsy Association, which has its headquarters in London.

A major function of the Council of World Organizations Interested in the Handicapped is to assist the non-governmental organizations in its membership in effectively relating to and whenever possible utilizing the services of the United Nations and its Specialized Agencies—in particular, UNESCO, the World Health Organization, the International Labor Organization, the United Nations Children's Fund, and, particularly with reference to the "developing" countries, the FAO—the Food and Agriculture Organization. Within the United Nations itself the Social Development Division is playing an important role, particularly through the work of its Unit on Rehabilitation of the Disabled; it is that Unit which is authorized to call together each year the UN Ad-Hoc Committee on Rehabilitation of the Disabled. During recent years mental handicap has received increasing attention from this group, which maintains a continuing relationship with CWOIH.

As we meet in our travels with agencies and their professional staffs, but also with colleagues from the academic field, my husband and I note with great regret how few people know of the excellent materials, documents, and significant policy declarations which emanate from these UN Agencies, and how little use is made of them, even where known. The highly developed industrialized countries are no exception.

In addition, there are of course important international regional organizations, such as the Council of Europe and the Organization of American States, whose resources are also under-utilized.

In the area of international cooperation there is a further resource which is very much underused, and that pertains to internationally sponsored exchange of students and practitioners, and to visits by consultants (many of them UN sponsored), or to study trips such as those based on grants like the Churchill Travel fellowships. All too often the results of these studies are not shared with a larger group, and excellent reports are limited to casual private circulation. As so often, the problem lies in the expense of organizing such materials for wider distribution, but merely the availability of such information as to who has been where would be most helpful, judging from the many requests for information which reach us personally.

One area in which the International League of Societies for the Mentally Handicapped has been particularly active in recent years, and which was the subject of one of its recent conferences in Brazil, is manpower and manpower training.

The concept of mental retardation, in its social, biological, and psychological dimensions, has undergone, during the past quarter century, most sweeping changes. Previous notions of the mentally retarded as a socially dangerous group, notions of the fixed I.Q. as a roadblock to substantial improvement, of the social incapacity of mentally retarded persons and of the ineducability of a large number of them, stood in the way of an aggressive program of training, treatment, and rehabilitation. With mental retardation thus conceived, there was little need for well trained, effective staff.

Today a totally different situation prevails. There is great emphasis on the educability of mentally retarded persons, on their capacity for growth and development, for learning and for continued application of what has been learned, their reaching out, and, in a growing number of cases, on their successful adjustment in the community; all this has both resulted in and is the result of a more dynamic approach to the problem of mental retardation.

To make international comparisons in an area of human services is always fraught with danger because so many underlying differences in culture and social technology need to be considered. However, one general observation pertains to the seeming variety and even contradictory nature of manpower development in the field of mental retardation during those 25 years. On the one hand, there is a definite trend towards acquisition of higher level training, a requirement for more specific academic qualification. On the other hand, there has been an interesting emphasis on using workers who have not had extensive training or academic qualifications but whose main strength lies in their ability to come close to the retarded person under care, and whose capacity lies not so much in an intellectual understanding of the many facets of mental retardation but in an intuitive ability to relate to, communicate with, and motivate retarded individuals. On closer scrutiny, these two trends do not turn out to be in conflict with each other but rather refer to quite different, separate functions which complement each other.

A third dimension refers to two additional sources of manpower. The one are the volunteers, often young or elderly persons, interested in helping their fellowmen. The other additional manpower source, at first accepted with great misgivings, are parents of retarded children. In an increasing number of countries they have been given an opportunity to participate actively in a large variety of programs; thus they have become members of what once was described restrictively as the professional team.

Among the established professional groups, education is undoubtedly taking the leadership in developing manpower for the field of mental retardation. In many countries this training originally was quite separate and apart, and usually privately arranged, such as that of teachers for more severely retarded children who were excluded from public schools and banished to so-called training centers, day care centers, and so forth. However, not only are classes for these children now part of an overall mental retardation program in an ever increasing number of countries, but more and more there is being developed a basic curriculum for teachers of all handicapped children, with specialization in the later stages of training. This relates also to the recognition that no child is "ineducable," and that every child should be considered from an individual developmental viewpoint.

In the process there has been a change in the perception of the role of teachers. In the past they often were limited to classroom duties; other so-called "clinical" persons were charged with studying the children and arriving at a diagnosis and plan of treatment. The acceptance of teachers as members of the clinical team has been very slow, yet when it came to the implementation of the recommendation of the clinical team, the teacher became the main actor. Together with a greater appreciation of their contribution has come in many countries an improvement of their salary and in the general status of the teachers of special education. This again has resulted in (or has in part resulted from) an increasing international communication between teachers of mentally retarded children, and, more broadly, special education teachers in general. There now exists the European Association for Special Education, and it is not hard to predict that in the near future we shall see a world-wide organization. There is reason to hope that such an international group will become affiliated with the World Confederation of Organizations of the Teaching Professions, which last year for the first time held a seminar on handicapped children and youth.

Education is one of the fields where personnel not meeting the traditional standards of professional preparation are playing a significant but as yet inadequately explored role. They are teacher aides, whose original function was limited to relieving the teacher of the time-consuming and, to many of them, unpleasant and "unprofessional" task encountered when incontinent or untidy children are admitted to a class group. In various countries we observed instances where the activities of these aides had progressed from a mere job of cleaning up and taking children to the toilet to a sharing of the educational task. They were able, for instance, under proper direction, to keep a group of children suitably occupied so that the teacher could work more intensively with an individual child requiring special attention. In other words, there was a reversal of the pattern which had been anticipated. On the other hand, we also observed instances where the aide would give individual attention and emotional support to a child who was particularly disturbed, perhaps even removing him from the classroom for a quieting walk. The main point I wish to make is that, in this as in other situations, workers with relatively limited formal training, working in conjunction with and supervised by a qualified teacher, can add substantially to the quality of the learning experience in the classroom.

In a few cases we observed how through a close cooperative relationship between the special class teacher and the teacher of a regular class of older children, a small group of these non-handicapped children, at their own request, guided play activities of individual handicapped children—always, of course, under proper direction. Language stimulation or some specific sensory motor activity was at times included.

In the nursery schools, of course, mothers of the children frequently participate in the educational process, as has long been a requirement in cooperative nursery schools and playgroups.

Altogether, parent participation in programs for mentally handicapped children is seen with increasing frequency, and this has added a new, enriching dimension to the manpower picture in the field of mental handicap. In several countries, selected parents have been trained to perform a function variously described as parent resource person, pilot parent, or visiting parent. Their task is to contact families where the problem of mental handicap has recently arisen and to provide emotional support, as well as specific information designed to encourage parents to utilize existing clinical, counseling, and auxiliary services, and to encourage parents to focus on meeting the needs of the child. At times such programs are managed independently by parent associations, but we have been in communities where physicians have accepted this arrangement as a valuable service which they can and do recommend. Parents also play in some parent education group programs the role of group leader. In France the parent-to-parent support program is well developed throughout the country under the name "Action Familiale"—or inter-family action, the translation used in a symposium on the subject held under the auspices of the International League of Societies for the Mentally Handicapped in 1972.

In Britain the National Society for Mentally Handicapped Children is promoting, through its regional organization, parent-to-parent support programs, and mention must also be made of the parent education demonstration programs undertaken by the Hester Adrian Research Centre at the University of Manchester.

It has not been possible for us to get an adequate picture of the many changes which are presently under consideration and in various stages of formulation in Britain, as far as manpower training of basic personnel working with mentally handicapped individuals in the area of health and social services is concerned. We do know that the results will be carefully evaluated in other countries where similar needs are felt but no such large scale efforts have been mounted. We would like to make one particular comment here that invites, we hope, controversy. It seems to us that some of the traditional training programs for institutional personnel, which originated during a period when there was little appreciation of developmental concepts and when maintenance of orderly routines of care was emphasized, result in staff attitudes— even among younger, newly trained workers—which reject a more dynamic, individualized approach.

Finally, there are definite indications that in the future we will see a new role for the handicapped individuals themselves. Sweden, already in 1973, issued a directive prescribing that every mental retardation service meet periodically with the clients, the retarded people themselves, to provide opportunity for them to participate in decision making insofar as this is feasible. In the words of the directive, the purpose is to stimulate individuals to participate actively in the shaping of their own situation and circumstances.

Even to some seasoned workers, expecting judgments of this nature from retarded individuals appears quite unrealistic. Yet elsewhere we have reported on the Mohawks, a social club of mentally retarded young men in Boston, Massachusetts, in existence for some ten years. More recently this group of young retarded people has successfully offered their services, for a modest fee, to provide consultation to organizations planning projects such as a sheltered workshop, hostel, or community residence.

Client participation is known in the field of rehabilitation as co-management. Enabling mentally retarded persons to have a voice in decisions affecting their daily living may seem to have little relevance to a discussion of the manpower situation. Yet when such participation leads to lessened dependence on staff and, at least for some, results in the ability to live in unsupervised apartments (as is already the case in some countries), the relevance should become clear.

Chapter 2

The Role Of
Voluntary Organizations*

When I started to think about the topic of today's meeting, my mind took me back about ten years to the League's Symposium in Lisbon, Portugal, on the development and operation of national societies and their relationship to the International League. We considered how the League could encourage and strengthen such national societies, what their problems were, and what kind of challenges presented themselves. In a paper prepared for that meeting I pointed out some of the highlights in the development of our associations during the preceding decade, in fact the first decade of the League's existence.

Among these were the following:

1. There had been a growing recognition that the mentally handicapped child was not a "child forever," but, like all other human beings, grew up to become an adult. In addition to changes in the specific programs the associations offered, this, just then, was causing League members to drop the word "children" from their name. We were becoming conscious of the inadequacy or inappropriateness of certain other words we were using. Even though the League had adopted two years earlier our Declaration of General and Special Rights of the Mentally Retarded, its full meaning had not yet been absorbed in the mainstream of the League members' thinking and vocabulary.

---

* *Eighth World Congress on Mental Retardation, Nairobi, Kenya, 1982*

2. I pointed out that the spectacular growth of some of our member societies had brought with it problems in the relationships and balance between the volunteers (the parents) and the professional staff in their respective roles in the administration of our societies.

3. My third point dealt with the need to bring new blood into the Society. What could be done to make room for younger parents?

4. I spoke also of the need for continued emphasis on what had been, from the very beginning, a main characteristic of our movement, the mutual aid directly from parent to parent, well exemplified by "Action Interfamiliale" then under development by UNAPEI, our French member society.

Since those days the League's member associations have made tremendous progress, but in some way or other the problems I then enumerated are still with us, and in at least some of the areas, it has been the very progress that has led to an accentuation and intensification of these questions.

I propose to use the traditional journalistic approach of *WHO*, *WHAT*, and *HOW* to describe the situation as I see it today. Furthermore, in view of the limited time available, I shall concern myself with the problems faced by the large metropolitan local associations of industrialized countries.

It is in the large local societies that we often find today a rift, a chasm between the old leadership group and the new members. In many cases our societies were started from within the upper middle class group, the well-to-do though not necessarily rich people. Their goals often resulted from a desire to obtain life time security for their children. The newer membership, often persons of lesser means, are seeking more limited, more immediate services. Furthermore, with few exceptions, our large metropolitan societies, which by sheer weight of numbers and financial resources have a powerful influence on the national organization, have failed to attract the underprivileged families who make up such a large proportion of a metropolitan population. Although this failure has been commented upon not infrequently, I have yet to see a study which deals with this crucial weakness in our organizational pattern in a meaningful way.

From my own visits to such large cities' associations, I would list as possible causes the setting and time of membership meetings, the traditional emphasis on association procedures (e.g., an agenda full of financial committee and sub-committee reports), and often also a guest speaker with a technical vocabulary that confuses rather than enlightens.

Increasingly we also observe a generational gap between the old leadership and the young families we wish to attract. This is not just a difference in age, but very much also a difference in needed services, and a difference in the general orientation to the problem of mental handicap; that is to say, in some areas the young families are more enlightened.

It is of course ironic that this more enlightened approach to mental handicap on the part of today's young families is the result of the successful efforts of our pioneers in providing educational information to the general public, and in overcoming old prejudices. I have rarely visited, in recent years, one of our large city associations, well staffed and rich in programs, which did not convey disappointment that so few "new" young parents could be recruited into membership (even from the parents who are using services provided by the association in a variety of aid programs).

Some years ago I observed with great satisfaction that many of our associations had started youth groups from among secondary school pupils or university students. It seemed to me that this was a most promising effort to recruit young people who could grow into leadership or who would in any case provide eventually useful indirect community support. However, recently I have observed and heard little along such lines. But I do remember well the valuable contribution of a member of such a youth group in Sweden attending a League symposium on volunteers in 1971.

Finally, in talking about the *WHO*, undoubtedly the greatest challenge to our associations comes from the persons with mental handicap themselves. After yesterday's exciting program, I do not need to spell out the significance of this self-advocacy movement further. It obviously is much easier for the League to arrange for participation of persons with handicap in a Congress like this, that takes place every four years, than for a long established large city association to work out meaningful participation or collaboration. I use the word collaboration because some of the groups which call themselves PEOPLE FIRST do seek an independent status rather than a formal membership arrangement.

Turning now to the *WHAT*, to the substance of the work of large city associations, the focal point today as always must be on the individuals with mental handicap and their families. Our new understanding of the developmental process of human growth as the mainspring of our activity presents new challenges. Traditional programming is no longer adequate in the light of a lifelong growth process that needs to be strengthened and supported for the disabled child from birth, and that is open-ended, that is to say, without fixed limitations once accepted as "realistic."

The new emphasis on early intervention has led to a rediscovery of the family. The emphasis is on bringing services for the handicapped infant and very young child *to the home*. This requires quite a shift in policy for societies that have developed a complex service system which serves the handicapped child *away* from home.

I am of course aware that there are associations which have done an exemplary job in this respect, but I see my task as pointing up problem areas that need attention and which the International League can help resolve through appropriate symposia, workshops, guidelines, and related materials.

How fast progress is made in our field is well exemplified in the area of early intervention, where we recognize the need of integrated services. Depending on circumstances, that may either be a program for many types of children with handicap, or, indeed, a general child health service.

On the other hand, changes must arise from our increasing understanding of the great importance of creating and reinforcing in young adults with handicap the awareness that they have grown out of childhood and must learn to enjoy their new status (and I should add here, of course, the words "in ways appropriate to their growth process").

To that extent, the comprehensive, all inclusive service complex developed by some of our large city associations needs to be *dis*-integrated so that adult services can be provided (as they usually are in our communities) separate and apart from those for children. And obviously this raises another and difficult question: What about the adolescent?

I am, of course, aware that large city associations with massive buildings and massive systems may not be numerous, but I do know of enough others which hope for and dream of the day when a benefactor or a new, generous government will enable them to have their own building complex with an extensive and comprehensive service system.

Turning now to the *HOW*, to procedural problems, the following points seem to be particularly germane to large city societies.

One relates to the style in which the association governs itself. Some of our large city associations have allowed themselves to grow to such proportion that they indeed constitute a major business enterprise, and that persuades them, of course, to hire business executives. Nobody should be surprised that this frequently results in an estrangement between the business managers, with their staffs, and the members—the parents. In other large city organizations one can observe a similar phenomenon: a highly qualified, properly certified staff, directed by an executive director who is also an outstanding professional. In the course of years this may easily result in a volunteer leadership on the board of directors which becomes so absorbed with professional services and all they entail that they themselves obtain almost professional status. But where, oh where, does that leave the general membership, old or new?

It is by no means a contradiction to emphasize the need for fruitful relationships with the relevant professional groups, because of the already mentioned trend towards *integrated* services, integrated across disabilities and disciplines. This would imply of course also a greater emphasis on specific fruitful relationships with parent associations representing different fields of handicap.

A major area of procedural and administrative problems relates to the financing. New developments in our field, related both to our much more positive outlook on mental disability and the potential of persons with handicap as well as our recognition of the rights of persons with handicap to respect and to dignity, put into serious question fund raising techniques which, in the past and right into the present, have played on the theme of "pity for the unfortunate" with great financial reward.

On the other hand, depending on government as a major source of large scale financing can lead to an unhealthy and inhibiting dependency on agencies which our societies should feel free to scrutinize and criticize. After all, you should not bite the hand that feeds you. To a lesser extent, any collaboration with government can become an impediment to a well developed association program when such collaboration in fact can be the power to "persuade" the association to concentrate on certain programs to the neglect of others. A similar danger would flow from the imposition of rigid standards that might be needed in a large bureaucracy, but which are inappropriate for a voluntary association that should be free to be flexible.

I commented earlier on the significance of words in our work, and that of course relates to terminology which has become outdated and which rightly causes anger and despair among persons who live with a mental handicap—I am sure that the panel of self-advocates we listened to yesterday morning could have given us some telling examples.

In closing, let me state quite clearly a bias I have with regard to the function of our societies. It is my belief that their task is to obtain services, not to provide them. Obtaining services quite frequently will involve one or more demonstration projects which may well last for several years, whether it is a program for severely and profoundly handicapped children, some innovative vocational training, or examples of new living arrangements in the community, for those who cannot or should no longer live with their family. And there are, of course, those important services which are inherent in the functioning of our societies, such as parent-to-parent counseling, continuing education of the public, and legislative action.

I am well aware that any proposal that will result in curtailing the income of an association will meet with much resistance. As always, the role of the International League will have to be to distribute relevant information about existing model programs, to provide workshops and seminars where these issues can be discussed in detail, and to make available position papers which will aid the leadership of national and local societies in charting their future.

Chapter 3

The International League of Societies for Persons with Mental Handicap*

It is my intention today to present to you the story of a large, international, non-governmental organization in the field of human services, the International League of Societies for Persons with Mental Handicap (ILSMHP): its origin; its composition and structure; its activities; some of the problems it faces; and a few thoughts about its future.

It was in the autumn of 1957 that my husband, then new Executive Director of the National Association for Retarded Children, requested me to help out with an accumulation of letters that had reached the Association from various foreign countries. Most were in English, some were not, and at that time the Association had no staff member available for this kind of correspondence. Little did I know that I was getting involved in an activity that would become my major professional (unpaid) concern over the next three decades.

At the end of World War II, of all the area in what we call today *Human Services*, none was as neglected in the terms of provision, none was as deficient in public knowledge, none had as low a standing in the academic world as the field of mental retardation, in those days referred to as mental deficiency, or feeble minded-ness, mental subnormality, or, in fancy scientific language, as oligophrenia. This is, of course, a broad generalization and there were exceptions, such as some good private institutions and some

---

* 1987

school systems which had classes for children with retarded mental development, or, in New York City, "low IQ classes." But overall, it was a largely negative picture.

For families, mental retardation was a matter of shame and guilt, *something to hide,* even from one's relatives. And this hiding not infrequently took on bizarre forms, such as children or adults chained in attics or basements.

Against this picture, in the years following the end of World War II, there occurred throughout the industrial world a phenomenon that has yet to be clearly understood in terms of its origin. In a broad cross-section of countries around the globe, small groups of parents began to get organized to protest against their retarded children's exclusion from schools and from all types of community activities. At the same time, many of the groups initiated, on their own, services such as schooling, recreation, and occupational activities.

Before 1950, local groups which were later to take on a national role were in existence in the USA, in England, France, and New Zealand; by 1953, when NARC's first Secretary, Mrs. Dorothy Moss, offered to act as an informal clearing house for the exchange of information and experiences, she was in touch with associations in Australia, Canada, Denmark, England, France, Israel, Japan, the Netherlands, New Zealand, Norway, and South Africa, and with individual parents or professional workers in Germany, India, Ireland, Mexico, Scotland, and the West Indies.

One might speculate about the driving force behind this spontaneous movement. It was started by no visible force; there were not then, nor were there to be for another decade, any international professional or voluntary organizations specifically active in the field of mental retardation. Nor were any of the United Nations Agencies to take more than a sporadic and limited interest, while programs of international organizations in mental health, child welfare, and education only rarely included any emphasis on mental retardation. It is important to point out that this early development occurred in widely separated countries with widely differing cultures. True, many of these starts were made in the English-speaking countries, Scandinavia, and the Netherlands, where there was a tradition of voluntary organization and cooperative self-help, but the second half of the 1950s saw a steady growth of beginnings in most other parts of the world.

In 1955, when NARC's International Relations Committee had been officially functioning for a year, a twenty-page bulletin was distributed by Mrs. Moss reporting on mental retardation programs, eleven of which by that time had national or federated parent-sponsored associations. By 1957, the Committee had active contacts with some forty countries, and two years later with sixty, twenty of which had national associations; in another twenty-four, one or more local groups were active.

There are some interesting parallels as to how these local groups got started and how they later developed into national organizations. In England, for instance, in 1947, Judith Frye, the mother of a severely retarded daughter, placed an advertisement in a magazine called *Nursery Times,* asking for contacts with any other mothers with similar problems. A year later Anne Greenberg placed an ad in the New York Post: "To the mothers of retarded children: Are you interested in forming a cooperative nursery school for your children?" A similar ad had been placed in the Bergen Evening Record by a mother in New Jersey. Interestingly, more than ten years later, Mrs. Nam Hong Choi in Korea had the same idea and placed a similar ad in a newspaper in Seoul. In each case, the advertisement led to establishment of a local group which developed a range of programs.

On the national level in some countries such as Argentina the driving force came from relatively unsophisticated parents, quite inexperienced in public life, whereas in neighboring Uruguay, it was a leading professional woman, principal of a special school, who pushed the national organization effort. In another South American country, Brazil, the impetus came from an American professor and his wife, themselves parents of a daughter with Down's Syndrome, who literally mobilized a nationwide effort in the 1950s, and who are still remembered with much appreciation by the founders of the National Federation of APAEs (Association of Parents and Friends of Exceptional Children) now composed of over 400 member branches. On the other hand, the national associations in Switzerland and Germany were initiated by people who had visited the National Association for Retarded Children in New York City, taking home information and inspiration.

Socialist countries in general frowned on voluntary organizations of almost any type and especially those with any trace of advocacy. In spite of this, a group of parents of mentally retarded children in Warsaw began meeting together in the late 1950s, and by 1963 had, with great skill, maneuvered themselves into acceptance as a semi-autonomous body within the child welfare organization, a tremendous achievement in those days of tight political control.

As was to be expected, the larger national organizations required administrative staff, and to this day the movement, first nationally and increasingly also locally, gives rise to a continuing dynamic interrelationship between the professional staff and the indigenous parent leadership. The fact that some of the parent leaders themselves had considerable professional standing made this interplay more intriguing.

When I came as a volunteer to NARC in 1957, I found that from its earliest beginnings, even before it had an office, NARC had developed an international outreach, primarily due to the indefatigable efforts of its secretary, Mrs. Dorothy Moss, of Cincinnati, Ohio. Although she herself had no professional training, nor international experience nor knowledge of a foreign language, she had followed up assiduously even the slightest reference to retardation in newspapers or journals or by word of mouth.

In 1954 the NARC president appointed its first International Relations Committee, with Mrs. Moss as chair. A year later she prepared a special 20-page bulletin entitled *Let's Get Acquainted*, which reported the activities in mental retardation programs in 22 countries, eleven of which by that time had some kind of national or federated parent-sponsored association. Without doubt, this was the first attempt to assess on an international basis the purpose and function of associations of parents.

In 1959 I began a series of international newsletters which were sent by NARC on a complimentary basis to parent organizations throughout the world as a means of stimulating further communication. Not surprisingly, we received at NARC Headquarters an ever-increasing volume of newsletters, brokers, and other materials from countries around the world, and, fortunately, in those days we were able to find a core of volunteers to assist in translation. A steady stream of visitors from other countries came to the New York Headquarters on NARC and in many cases we were able to direct them to resources and to other interested persons in their own and in neighboring countries. "Networking" was not yet a word in the English language, but it describes well the main thrust of NARC's International Committee.

1960 had been proclaimed World Mental Health Year. In Europe in particular, some of the parent associations had been in touch with the World Federation for Mental Health, and in March of that year an informal meeting of parent groups took place in The Hague to consider the possibility of organizing at an international level. The countries represented were Denmark, England, France, Germany, Greece, Italy, the Netherlands, and Switzerland. It must be remembered that by that time the Council of Europe, established in 1949, and the European Community, in 1951, were promoting a keen awareness of European solidarity. Hence, without disavowing an eventual international organization, the group drew up plans and a constitution, creating the European League of Societies for the Mentally Handicapped, which in October, 1962, held in London its first congress. In the following year the name of the group was changed to the International League of Societies for the Mentally Handicapped, and parent groups from throughout the world expressed interest in becoming affiliated.

Today, 26 years later, the International League has a total of 113 member societies, belonging to 76 countries, representing every continent, 53 being national member societies and 60 affiliated members.

Wilhelm Busch, the 19th Century German humorist, has said:

"Vater werden ist nicht schwer,
Vater sein dagegen sehr."

(It's not hard to become a father,
But very hard to be one.)

The same might be said about a world-wide organization. With some wisdom, enthusiasm, and persuasion it is possible to create such a body, but to maintain it over decades on a truly international basis, that is another story. And yet there is no question that if we are to preserve the United Nations and its affiliated agencies, we must have world-wide citizens or nongovernmental organizations to support, to monitor, to guide, and to challenge the official United Nations system. Therefore, I would like to point out to you that what I am saying here today about the International League, to a large measure, would also apply to other international groups in which you might—or should—be interested, whether they are professional associations or associations in the field of the arts, sports, or mercantile or industrial groups.

I shall now present to you some comments on the legal status of the International League, try to give a picture of what it is actually doing, and then point up some of the serious obstacles it must overcome, with some final comments as to what the future might bring.

The League is an association organized under the laws of Switzerland, with Geneva as its principal seat. However, as permitted by the League's Constitution, its actual headquarters are in Brussels, Belgium. While the location in Brussels was originally an accommodation to the League's then General Secretary, it proved to be a fortunate choice since the city has become a major center for international activities. Article II of the Constitution says the following about purposes and means of the International League:

ARTICLE II
PURPOSES AND MEANS
SECTION I. The purposes of the League are:

a) To advance the interest of persons with mental handicap, without regard to nationality, race or creed, by securing on their behalf from all possible sources, the provision of remedial, residential, educational training, employment and welfare services.

b) To create a common bond of understanding among parents and families of the retarded and others affected by the problem of mental handicap throughout the world.

c) To promote the interest of persons with mental handicap and their families by bringing about cooperation among organizations representing national endeavour in their behalf.

SECTION 2. To carry out these purposes the League shall:

a) Promote the interchange of experts and information on the development of services for the mentally handicapped.

b) Foster the exchange of workers in the field of mental handicap between one country and another.

c) Undertake the comparative study of legislation in member countries and beyond, relative to persons with mental handicap, and the provision of services for their well-being.

d) Encourage the formation and development of national societies in the interest of persons with mental handicap in all countries; assist and stimulate them through the exchange of information and the experiences of others, the better to cope with the needs of their own mentally handicapped; engender in such organizations and in their members an awareness of the necessity and importance of their joining in an international effort to accomplish the welfare of the mentally handicapped the world over.

e) Cooperate with other international organizations, both governmental and voluntary, in advancing the welfare of persons with mental handicap and in promoting the scientific research and professional training necessary thereto.

f) Receive, use, hold and apply any contributions, bequests of endowments, or the proceeds thereof, in advancing the welfare of persons with mental handicap.

g) Employ such other means as the Assembly and Council of the League shall from time to time determine.

Let me now turn to an actual accounting of the activities the League is carrying on, pursuant to the Constitution. By far the most engrossing and most productive activity is the organization of the League's quadrennial World Congresses on Mental Retardation and the biannual Assemblies taking place midway between the Congresses. As a consumer organization, the League has definitely geared its congresses to the interests and needs of its membership. They do not offer the often overwhelming and unfortunately highly ineffectual potpourri of parallel sessions on a myriad of unrelated topics characteristic of so many international conferences organized to a large extent to accommodate the needs of the presenters rather than those of the audience. Instead, the League has worked out a basic format which combines major plenary sessions in the morning, with discussion groups related to the plenary session topic, followed in turn by small workshops on selected sub-topics. While the plenary session has simultaneous translation in four languages, the smaller discussion groups may be divided by language groupings, whereas most of the workshops will be in one language only. A great deal of thought is given to select an overall Congress theme with a sub-theme for each day. Let me give you just one example: The 7th World Congress held in 1978 in Vienna had as its main theme Choices *and Learning to Choose,* in recognition of the beginning emancipation of individuals with mental retardation as persons in their own right. Thus the theme of the first day was "Choices for People Who Are Mentally Retarded"; for the second day, "Choices for the Family"; for the third day, "Choices in Partnership" (i.e., the partnership of parents and professionals); and, for the fourth day, "Choices for Society," i.e., the broad problems of legislation, policy, and service systems (ISLMH, 1978a).

Only a small number of persons with mental retardation were actually in attendance, but four year later, at the World Congress in Nairobi, Kenya, you might say we moved from theory to practice because we had in attendance more than 50 persons with mental retardation, representing eight different countries. One of the four plenary session was organized by that group. They presented a panel discussion chaired by one of them, and subsequently responded to unrehearsed questions put to them by the audience with the help of the official interpreters. The general theme of that Congress was *Partnership*, followed in 1986 at the Congress in Rio de Janeiro by the theme, *Mental Handicap—A Challenge for All:* Together *We Can Do It*, attended by some 1200 people from 70 countries, including some 200 persons with mental retardation. The last day in Rio had the theme *Meeting the Challenge—We Can Be Partners.* Since the Nairobi Congress in 1982, all over the world people with mental handicaps have been encouraged to think positively about themselves and matters of interest to them.

Next to the congresses in importance are symposia and workshops. They are small, invitational meetings of no more than 40 participants, with theme or position papers prepared and distributed in advance. One of the most important of them took place near Stockholm in 1967 on the subject "Legislative Aspects of Mental Retardation"(ILSMH, 1967a). Part III of the Conclusions of that Symposium dealt with individual rights, and was so clearly and powerfully worded that the following year at the League's 4th Congress in Jerusalem, on the theme "From Charity to Rights," it was decided to adapt and adopt the text as a Declaration of the General and Special Rights of the Mentally Retarded. Nobody, absolutely nobody, would or could have foreseen that only three years later, on the initiative of the Government of France, this Declaration would be adopted, first by the Economic and Social Council, and then by the full United Nations Assembly, without a dissenting vote. Here you have a very clear example of the potential inherent in the work of non-governmental organizations within the United Nations system. It goes without saying that it was UNAPEI, the League's member society in France, that caused the French government to take the initiative of placing this Declaration on the Economic and Social Council's agenda.

To demonstrate further the interplay between the United Nations Organization and the International League as an NGO (non-governmental organization), let me add that after the UN had promulgated this so important declaration, the League appointed a guide entitled Step by Step: Implementation of the Rights of Mentally Retarded Persons, *which*, printed in four languages, provides some analytical guidelines for member societies (ILSMH,

1978b).

There is one further point worth noting. When the League became aware that there was a good likelihood for the adoption of its Declaration of Rights by the United Nations, it suggested to the staff of ECOSOC that it would be advantageous to extend the Declaration to persons with other handicaps. The staff, however, disagreed, and pointed out that since there was a good chance of early adoption by the Assembly, broadening the Declaration to include other handicaps would necessitate lengthy consultations with the large number of NGOs, with the likelihood of disagreement as to terminology and the like. On the other hand, suggested the staff, once a Declaration had actually been adopted on behalf of persons with mental retardation, the other disability groups would do everything to facilitate a second, more broadly-gauged Declaration. This proved to be exactly correct, and only four years later (a very brief period in international workings), a Declaration of the Rights of Disabled Persons was adopted by the United Nations General Assembly. I presented to you this story in some detail because it so clearly illustrates the workings of the United Nations and the non-governmental organizations.

The third major area of the League's functioning deals with the work of committees. A good number of them concern obvious administration aspects of the League. Others deal with such subjects as, in alphabetical order, Aging; Behavioral Concerns; Integrated Education; Leisure and Social Life; Mobilization of Resources; Participation of Persons with Mental Handicap; Prevention' Profound Handicap; Rights and Advocacy; and Work Opportunities. The foregoing three aspects of the League's work, the Congresses, the Symposia, and the Committee work, all contribute substantially to the League's production of printed materials, primarily pamphlets and leaflets, suitable for mass distribution. It will not surprise you to hear that the League does not have sufficient funds to publish all its material in its four "official" languages (English, French, German, and Spanish), thus creating another area of difficult decision making.

My next point regarding the League's agenda, namely, work with other organizations, might well have been given a higher priority. There we have in first place the United Nations and its so-called "Specialized Agencies," particularly the World Health Organization, the International Labor Organization, UNESCO, and the Food and Agriculture Organization. Within the United Nations proper, the League is accredited to the Economic and Social Council as well as to UNICEF. Accreditation as a NGO to the United Nations or to any of its specialized agencies carries with it the right to attend meetings and assemblies of those bodies, the right to submit position papers and proposals, and, at certain, specified times, the right to speak.

Alongside the United Nations family are other agencies such as the Organization of American States and its Interamerican Children's Institute, located in Montevideo, the Council of Europe, the European Community, and the Organization of Economic Cooperation and Development (OECD) and its Center for Educational Research and Innovation (CERI), located in Paris. Finally, the League must interact with international Non-Governmental Organizations such as Rehabilitation International, the International Association for the Scientific Study of Mental Deficiency, the International Catholic Children's Bureau (in Paris and Geneva), and the International Council on Disability (formerly known as CWOIH), a coordinating body of NGOs in the broad field of rehabilitation which interfaces with the United Nations Interagency Committee on Rehabilitation of the Disabled. Overall, this is a most formidable job of networking. Some of you experience much frustration in trying to keep in touch on a functional basis with eight other agencies right here in this community, and there seem to be insurmountable obstacles to statewide patterns of collaboration and information exchange. Yet, on the international scene you have to deal with sister organizations on other continents (Rehabilitation International is headquartered in New York, the League in Brussels, the Catholic Child Bureau in Paris), which means that as the executive in New York comes to work in the morning, her counterpart in Europe is getting ready to leave his office—and what about that urgent telephone call to your vice-president in Japan?

In my listing of League activities I now come to a new undertaking which has been met with much interest (if not enthusiasm), in spite of great difficulties in implementation. As is obvious within the League membership, we have striking differences with regard to the human, financial, and professional resources available to the various associations. Thus a plan was developed to make possible some exchange between national associations. The plan was initiated at the 1982 Nairobi Congress with a so-called Partnership Market. Associations from Third World countries were encouraged to spell out specific needs that an association in an industrial country might provide, such as a visit by a consultant, an apprenticeship, or specific materials, books, and the like. Conversely, the better situated associations were encouraged to offer some services. As yet this project has grown very slowly, but its most tangible result so far has been a heightened awareness of the need and the possibility of such a program of sharing. Interestingly, already at the first Partnership Market in Nairobi, some African countries worked out such an arrangement among themselves with some consultative and financial assistance from the Norwegian Association. The Scandinavian associations have been generous in such help, in Asia as well as Africa, and the German Lebenshilfe has given outstanding help, with direct participation from many of its local associations in hosting staff from Asian countries for periods of study and observation.

Let me bring this listing of League activities to an end by mentioning that in recent years the Committee on Rights and Advocacy has submitted, on behalf of the League, legal briefs as amicus curiae, in lawsuits of international significance; that a periodic newsletter goes to members, published in four different languages; that the Headquarters office maintains a multi-lingual information and referral service.

I hardly need to emphasize to you that trying to maintain an international organization such as the League involves a host of problems. The League wants to be, of course, a democratic organization, and has fashioned a very open process of nominations and elections for the officers and executive council (13 persons). The point is, unfortunately, that the more representative the Council is, i.e., the more widespread geographically, the harder it is to bring people together for meetings. At present, the League pays for half of the travel expenses of the Council and officers, but even half fare may be far too expensive for a small association in a Third World country. Another approach to the problem of running a world-wide organization is having regional vice-presidents; next, regional committees were developed by the League, beginning with a very active European Committee. In similar fashion the African manner associations have created "Network Africa," with help in the beginning from Norway and Sweden.

The actual day-by-day administration of the League is in the hands of an Administrative Director. Very purposefully the term Executive Director was avoided to prevent what so easily happens, the gradual assumption by the headquarters staff of greater power and responsibility. An additional safeguard in that respect is the establishment by the Constitution of an elective post of Secretary General to whom the Administrative Director reports. The League has been fortunate in maintaining a good working balance in this respect, largely because the very capable, long-time Administrative Director is content with this arrangement.

Selection of a headquarters is a particularly difficult problem for an international organization. On the one hand, it is expected to have a "prestigious" office in terms of the location, furnishings, and so forth. On the other hand, it operates on a very small overseas budget, in striking contrast to those of its member societies, who run large programs from which they gain large overhead. Furthermore, inevitably an international organization has members from poor countries which can barely afford the membership dues, even though those are prorated. For many years the League operated from a 4th floor walk-up attic office, and this conservative approach helped to stabilize the League's finances at a time when other organizations faced a sudden and very disruptive retrenchment.

Another challenge that affects the League's publications as much as its day-to-day operations is terminology. There are tremendous differences from country to country, and terms like "subnormal," which is considered highly offensive in some countries, are still in regular use in others. Terminology also affected the name of the organization, which was changed a few years ago from League of Societies for the Mentally Handicapped to League of Societies for *Persons* with Mental Handicap. There has been also much discussion about the suitability of the adjective "mental," which to most people conveys an association with mental illness. The New Zealanders, for example, have always used the term Intellectual Handicap, and the Australians are now joining this trend, keeping their initials AAMR but defining their official name as Australian Association for the Intellectually Disabled. Some people find a distinction between the connotations of the words association and society; and the word "advocacy" presents a challenge to translators into the romance languages, where its meaning is strictly a legal one. This listing could go on interminably. Agreements are often reached only after long discussions and apparent compromises all around.

A few years ago the League had a symposium in Madrid on "The Future of Voluntary Association." Thirty-six persons from 22 countries participated. The following excerpts from the report of this symposium, prepared by Ann Shearer of the Campaign for Mentally Handicapped People (London), will show you, I believe, how similar the concerns voiced at the symposium are to problems and concerns of associations in our own country.

The symposium's general and pragmatic conclusion was that there can be no hard and fast rules, that the role of associations would depend very much on the circumstances in which they found themselves. But that leaves some unanswered questions:

Questions of responsibility:
If associations are to continue to provide services, how far are they to prepare to go in this?

If the task of the 1980s is to translate selected demonstration programmes into broad and general ones, are associations willing to take full responsibility for this? If so, they will become massive bureaucracies indeed! What would then happen to their role as advocates for and supporters of parents and people with mental handicaps, when they themselves have so clearly become "the boss"? If not, how will the responsibility be shared: Are some services best run by government and others best run by the associations?

Already in some countries a trend is apparent: voluntary associations on the whole [provide] good community services for people whose handicaps are moderate and severe, while government runs on the whole bad services in institutions for people whose handicaps are multiple and profound. This in inequitable. It also means that the people who need the most help get the least. Is this trend to become even more pronounced? If responsibility is to be shared among many voluntary associations, who is to coordinate the services provided? How are standards to be maintained?

Questions of quality:
The symposium concluded that it is possible for associations to be both providers of services and advocates, change agents and monitors or quality. But there are unanswered questions here too.

- How can an association credibly advocate for improvements in government services unless it is sure that its own services are as good as they possibly could be? How does it ensure that?

- How far does it systematically take account of the views of service users—parents of children and people with mental handicaps themselves?

- What objective standard is it using to assess its own services?

- What happens when parents or people with mental handicaps have a complaint against the association's services? To whom do they turn when their "advocates" have become the enemy? What systems of external monitoring are backing the association's own internal efforts to ensure quality?

- What happens when an association which is largely funded by government wants to criticize government services? Is it strong enough to bite the hand that feeds it? And is the hand strong enough to take it—without retaliating by cutting funds or denying the association its place on consultative bodies?

In summing up the symposium, Ann Shearer said the following:

> As rapporteur, I am left with a predominant image of associations working against indifference and even hostility from the world "out there." We heard more of the difficulties and doubts of association—in their very different settings and stages of development—than we did about their very considerable achievements.
>
> That's not, perhaps, surprising. The purpose of the seminar was, after all, not to celebrate the positives of past and present, but rather to try to chart a way ahead into times which look to be both difficult and problematic. Many of the people from the "developed" countries, too, brought with them a whole historical baggage of hard struggle to establish and maintain their associations—and that is bound to colour how they live the present and anticipate the future. For the people from "developing" countries, that struggle is most often the present reality. Even in "developed" countries where associations are strong and well-established, there is no shortage of battles to be fought in these hard economic times. The call to arms becomes both a necessity and an obvious rallying cry. . . .
>
> So as ILSMH's members look towards their future, is there perhaps the need for not just a greater openness to the possibilities of that wider world, but a keener set of strategies for reaching into it and a different balance between looking inwards to their associations' own needs and looking outwards to potential new alliances? And is there too the need for a sharper understanding of the nature of the battles to be fought—battles which have to do with the balance of power and influence among and between organizations rather than among and between individuals? (Shearer, 1985)

PART II

Prevention and Intervention

Chapter 4

Prevention and Intervention in England: A 1975 Perspective[*]

Six weeks of intensive discussion in Britain with professional workers from the fields of education, health, and social service in local and state agencies, both public and private, as well as with individual parents of mentally handicapped children, make it fairly obvious that the decisive changes which had been expected as a consequence of the radical reordering of statutory and administrative provisions in the field of mental handicap have fallen far short of expectations. Many of our colleagues seem to feel that the process of change has slowed down to a point where it barely can hold its own against the ever present force the sociologists call "system maintenance," the inherent reaction of administrative bodies and their staffs to resist change which is threatening established work patterns, procedures, and privileges.

We are, of course, aware of the statement of the Secretary of State for Health and Social Security of February 26, 1975, in which she acknowledged, in essence, her Department's disappointment with this state of affairs, and in which she announced the appointment of a National Development Group for the Mentally Handicapped which is to play an active role in the development of departmental policy and the strategy for its implementation. This is therefore a very propitious time to put forth suggestions which focus as sharply as possible on what could be seen as possible reasons for the failure of the programs outlined in earlier government documents. I would like to discuss with you what my husband and I consider to be one of the crucial elements in this

[*] *Castle Priory College, Wallingford, England, 1975*

failure, namely, the neglect of the needs of mentally handicapped infants and young children and their families.

As we have talked with colleagues in the various disciplines concerned with mental handicap in various localities over the past six weeks, we have of course become aware of the intensity of the argumentations for or against the continued use of the large institution, for or against community residences, for or against integration, for or against segregated schools, for or against creating work opportunities for mentally handicapped adults on the open labor market. Much of this argumentation seems to us to be fundamentally in error because it is based on judgments of the potential of mentally handicapped children and adults which have been derived from the very conditions of past neglect and ignorance we are seeking to overcome in the future.

Just two months ago at a workshop attended by professional people, a person who questioned present proposals for social integration of mentally handicapped adults because of the potentially embarrassing situations it might cause cited as an example a young woman with Down's Syndrome "throwing her arms enthusiastically around people." While this kind of behavior unfortunately can still be observed all too frequently, it has of course long been proven that this simply is the result of misguided upbringing. Educational procedures to prevent this kind of social conduct have long been established and proven themselves.

I hope that during the discussion period some of you will point to similar instances where some of our colleagues base the programming for the future on the results of the misjudgment and the mismanagement of the past, but time commands me to address myself to the key point of my presentation, the neglect of the needs of the mentally handicapped infant and young child.

Let me quote from the findings of a conference on early programming which are about to be published.

> The provision of a suitable programme of care for the mentally handicapped child and his family warrants serious consideration. There are two aspects to this problem; first, the urgent and crucial matter of how best to break the news to the parents; secondly, how best to supply the emotional and practical support which families are likely to need in the

years to come. The evidence suggests that on both counts we are failing markedly at present to provide the kind of service which families require. (Spain and Wigley, 1975)

Similarly, at last year's annual meeting of the Association of Professions for the Mentally Handicapped, entitled "Better Services—the Realities," Kenneth Holt, pediatrician-in-chief of the Wolfson Centre, stated that "so far as the early detection of developmental delay and retardation symptoms is concerned, none of the medical services available is really satisfactory." (Holt, 1974)

But, of course, the most eloquent testimony about this situation would come from parents, particularly those with severely multiply handicapped children who in all too many instances still today are left without good, common sense practical help: assistance that would aid them in managing their children and meeting their developmental needs in the very first few years of life, and that would, it has long been shown, very substantially improve the level of their children's functioning.

We are dealing here with a very strange phenomenon. The dynamic change in the way in which mentally handicapped people are perceived in your country (and through you in many others) can be traced back very clearly to the pioneering work with mentally handicapped adults as demonstrated by Ann and Alan Clarke, Tizard, Gunzburg, and others.

Gradually, all too gradually, the recognition of the surprising level of performance of quite severely mentally handicapped adults led to a reassessment of educational procedures. At long last the myth of the ineducable child was laid to rest when it was discovered that the problem was not with the children "who could not learn" but rather with the teachers who did not know how to teach them. However, it looks as if progress in education is proceeding at a rather slower speed as compared with that in the vocational and work area, and we would suggest that the reason for that is at the very root of this developmental phenomenon; namely, that our developmental sequence of services was in reverse, that we are moving last where we should have started— namely, with the mentally handicapped infant and very young children, their needs, their potentials, and the services which will respond to their needs and develop their potential.

In other words, the proposition which we are putting up for debate this morning is of deceptive simplicity and goes like this: families with severely mentally handicapped children, and particularly those with multiply handicapped children, are apt to encounter a broad range of problems which I shall specify later in my presentation. In the past we have failed to give parents effective aid with these problems, with the result that the situation over the years became more and more aggravated, and both parents and children needlessly suffered. Therefore we recommend a basic shift in policy, giving a high priority to a range of services which will aid the child and support the parent in the home.

It is a very simple and clear recipe. As I shall show, it does not involve the spending of large amounts of money, does not require construction of buildings, and can be implemented with knowledge and techniques available today. As a matter of fact, in bits and pieces, components of a program of early intervention have already been practiced in various parts of this country for a good number of years. Yet it is very clear that the writers of the White Paper, *Better Services for the Mentally Handicapped* (Department, 1972), and of subsequent government documents have failed to recognize this problem in its practical aspects as a key issue and have failed to set the stage for the implementation of programs of early intervention, notwithstanding some broad statements about needed support to the home.

By the way, I am aware that early intervention is a term objected to be some people as implying too much intrusion. It needs to be understood as being put into opposition to the attitude of laissez-faire, the benign neglect which has characterized the early years of the mentally handicapped infant within the home.

A great deal has been written in professional literature about the psychological problems of parents with severely mentally handicapped children. An example is this excerpt from the report of a very recent conference: "All parents with severely handicapped children suffer severe stress in acute form when the handicap is recognized, and in a more chronic form of depression and anxiety later. It is important that this is recognized and informal psychiatric screening should be done on all families with handicapped children." We are very weary of this glib general reference to the need for psychiatric help. It is of course entirely to be expected that parents faced with the birth of a severely handicapped child have a reaction of deep disappointment and grief. But as we know from numerous testimonies of parents, they also have a sense of great frustration because they do not understand what has happened and what the future will be. More positively stated, parents want to understand what is wrong with their child *and what they can do to help him or her*. When they are frustrated in this, and this frustration persists, they indeed will become disturbed.

The initial problem of course relates to the way in which parents are being told that they have a mentally handicapped child, because all too often the negative attitude of the informant sets off a negative chain reaction in the parent. This is exemplified in the phrase, "There is nothing that can be done."

Admittedly this important process of first informing the parents is hard to control, but what must give us great concern is that the much more formalized, elaborate process of assessment which occurs much later still continues to be handled frequently in a very unsatisfactory way, as far as the parent is concerned. Within the past month, Ann Jones, a psychologist, very forcefully pointed out in an article in *New Psychiatry* (April 24, 1975) that much of the value of assessment is lost because its real meaning is not conveyed to the parents in a comprehensible form. As a result, instead of gaining an understanding of what is wrong with their children and what kind of help they need, the parents get irritated, frustrated, and disturbed. Ann Jones makes a very simple, practical suggestion—that the parents get a detailed, comprehensible, *written* report of the assessment.

This very sensible suggestion is by no means obviated by another recommendation that has been made by many parent associations in various countries, but recently has been echoed by a few professional persons and indeed in a very few places been put into practice—that the parents be given an opportunity to participate in the assessment process and in particular in the assessment conference, unless some unusual circumstances speak against that.

Furthermore, because experience has brought out very clearly that an initial assessment cannot possibly predict with accuracy the child's development, periodic reassessment with participation from the parents, but perhaps with a more limited professional staffing, is of the essence. What needs to be stressed is that in distinction to the term "diagnosis," the term "assessment" should be understood to include a statement of the child's needs and ways of meeting them, and each time, we agree with Ann Jones, the parents should get a written summary.

The process of assessment is usefully supplemented by parent education of the type so successfully demonstrated by the staff of the Hester Adrian Centre at the University of Manchester. Parents of a severely handicapped child come face to face with new words like mental handicap and mental subnormality, new facilities like day center or special care center, new procedures like speech stimulation or motor development; experience has shown they can learn best about these things if they are being discussed in a group, although we must of course make allowance for the occasional parent for whom participation in a group is either undesirable or inappropriate. Much is gained when parents have a better under- standing not just of their handicapped child's special needs, but to what extent that child is more like than unlike other children.

Parent education in groups is usually organized for a limited number of meetings. It is, as the name says, an educational process, and needs to be clearly differentiated from parent counseling, which may take place either individually or also in groups. Parent education conveys broad information; parent counseling deals with specific problem situations the parent is encountering with the management of the child, in the relationship with neighbors, in the use of community facilities.

The essence of early intervention, of course, lies in making available to parents not only advice and counsel but detailed technical instruction or perhaps specific equipment that will help them in taking care of their children and furthering their growth and development. From our own experience with many parents, we know, for instance, that feeding such a child may pose great problems, taking hours of the mother's time and causing her great anxiety. Yet there are simple ways of helping the mother to teach her child to suck, to swallow, to use a spoon, and they can easily be demonstrated. I had hoped to show you as one example a brief teaching film on such a subject, but technical problems made this not possible.

Many mothers urgently need not only to understand the nutritional requirements of their child but ways to meet them, need to understand not only the sequence from soft to solid food but how to achieve this, need to understand the significance of proper food and proper chewing, not just for dentition but for the beginnings of language development. Parents struggle needlessly with feeding problems when a special spoon, a special cup, or some other procedure may speed up the training, not only saving the parent time but helping child and parent to move on to the next developmental stage. Add to this effective help with sleep problems and toilet training, and the improvement in the domestic scene and the child's greater readiness for a first group experience will be advanced beyond measure.

That the first three years of life are the most significant development learning period in a child's life is common knowledge, yet traditionally we have thought of education as a business of schools. But education does of course begin at home, and the role of the parent as a teacher in child development is of particular significance with the handicapped child. For instance, a baby with Down's syndrome needs a maximum of stimulation, through early sensory training and in motor development. Short teaching films are available to show a mother how to help her baby with Down's syndrome to learn to raise his or her head, or to roll over. There is the matter of speech stimulation and development, and the all important need for parents to understand that the severely mentally handicapped child will need help in developing a concept of self. Managing such a child may require home help, and Britain has not only pioneered in providing home helpers but now also is providing an attendance allowance in consideration of the extra expenses which accrue to families with this kind of problem.

Multiply handicapped children have need for medical intervention, and our contacts with parents indicate this still today presents an uneven picture, particularly in terms of orthopedic and other needed surgery, eye glasses, and hearing aids, where help is often not offered, and if requested, refused. There is little recognition by many physicians even today that many of these children need special attention for problems which are well within reach of remedial medical steps.

For the latest documentation on this may I refer to the lead article in the *British Medical Journal* of April 12, 1975. Let me read in full the section dealing with Down's syndrome:

A mongol child aged 3 is seen. The diagnosis, already apparent from the child's appearance, should have been confirmed by chromosomal studies. If they have not been done they should be done now. Then the child and parents should be referred to a genetic clinic for counselling. If it is a heritable form of Down's syndrome, the parents, especially if they have other children, should know the probable risks for grandchildren.

There is no specific treatment for mongolism, but it is important that (a) the child gets the full value of available education, and (b) the parents get some relief from the burden of looking after the child. As regards the child, preschool education would be an advantage, starting with play group and then going to nursery school if available. The parents may be advised to persist in training the child in feeding, dressing, and use of toilet. The tendency is to be over protective, but the majority of mongols, given extended training, can learn these skills. In fact, given sufficient education, many children with Down's syndrome can learn to read and write.

The parents may need a holiday from the child. The present options are (1) residential centres provided by the social work department, (2) hospital (most hospitals take a large number of children and adults for an annual holiday), and (3) a holiday home run by a voluntary society (for example, the Society for Mentally Handicapped Children). Parents should be advised to join the local branch of the National Society for Mentally Handicapped Children. In many areas they run swimming clubs and hold children's play sessions. Dental care may be a problem. The alternatives have been discussed earlier in this paper.

Parents always want to plan for the distant future. In fact little need be done until the child is nearing the end of school life. Then the family doctor should either contact the social work department so that the family get support there or ask a consultant from the local mental handicap hospital to see the child and the parents with a view to advising on postschool management and to give an undertaking about later residential placement if this proves necessary.

You may feel that there is much good information in these paragraphs. That is correct, but it does not tell the general practitioner much that is helpful about the specific ways in which the physician can aid the physical development of a child with Down's syndrome. For that the parent still has to go to Mr. Brinkworth, a child psychologist, whose booklet *Improving Your Baby with Down's Syndrome* has been a landmark in the efforts to bring to parents helpful information for the earliest years.

I do want to acknowledge that at the APMH meeting in Nottingham last month a physiotherapist specifically commented on work with very young children. She said that "the earlier a handicap is noticed and treated the better. When a child is multiply handicapped this is obvious, but it has also been found that Down's babies improve with early physiotherapy and it is common for mentally handicapped children to have retarded motor development." The problem is that it takes a physician's initiative to mobilize the skilled help of the physiotherapist, and too many physicians do not see the need for this intervention.

There is no time for me to deal with the importance of telling the mother about the significance of play and the help that toy libraries and consultation centres can provide in this regard, or the importance of social contacts and of preparing a child gradually for being away from the familiar home environment and away from mother, significant learning preparation for joining a pre-school program.

I realize as I said at the beginning that most of these services are known to most of you. The question is, under what circumstances, if at all, are they available in your community? In other words, the problem of early intervention is largely a problem of *service delivery*.

One further comment: there is always much emphasis on prevention of mental retardation, but aside from broad scale measures such as improved maternal and child care, our capacity for primary prevention of severe subnormality is still very limited. Early intervention, on the other hand, can be a powerful tool in secondary prevention, in eliminating needless complications as a consequence of added disability.

One crucial element in the service delivery in this area of early intervention for mentally handicapped children is the problem of staffing. Who is to do the job? My husband and I have tried very hard over the past six weeks to gain an understanding of what the various reorganizational moves in state and local services have to suggest in this respect. I hope you don't mind our saying that we found no answer for this because none of the planners seems to have given the problem sufficient thought to provide an answer.

There is a need here to point to what impresses us as a basic weakness in your reorganization. We hasten to add that we invariably experience the same in our country with this type of reorganization. It is organized from the top down, instead of from the bottom up. It is structured to facilitate and safeguard the work of the bureaucrat rather than to give prime consideration to the citizen in need. Beautiful organization charts have been prepared that show the Secretary of State and the Department and the Region and the Area and the District, with a maze of interconnecting lines of responsibility and communication. But nowhere to be found are John and Mary Smith and their severely handicapped son, Billy.

My husband and I have visited, as consultants in mental retardation, some 35 countries, and of necessity we had to develop some approaches, some techniques, to assess the effectiveness of national systems of care. We, of course, studied the kind of organization chart I just described, which always would be handed to us, but then we tried to design a reverse chart, starting with the front line person, be she a health visitor, a recreation worker, the teacher in a day care centre, or a caseworker on a large ward in a large institution. From whom do they get guidance? Who monitors their work? And, a very important question for people we lock away in institutions, who is there to provide staff guidance and supervision and to monitor the programs over the long dreary weekend? The picture one gets in that way does look quite different from the organization chart.

The other technique we always utilize is to bring down the discussion to a specific case. For this we have a formula that can be used anyplace: It is, as the sociologists like to say, a culture-free test. We simply ask, "Suppose a child is born in your town or village tomorrow and is found to be severely handicapped, an infant with Down's syndrome, perhaps; or suppose the mother decides that she will no longer be put off by her physician who says her two-year old child will outgrow its obvious retardation, and she is looking for help: what does your town, your village have to offer to such a mother and to her child?"

Our third and often most vital approach is to turn to the consumer, to go to the parent. We are indebted to individual parents and the local societies of parents of mentally handicapped children and adults for so much of what we have learned in the last 15 years about the realities of mental handicap.

It is on this basis that we have been trying, during our present stay in England, to get a realistic picture of how the services connect with the parent client, or how the parents can connect themselves to the services. We are, of course, well aware that there are many excellent services in this country, services which have really set the tone for other countries, but this is not the question here. It is little comfort to the mother with a Down's syndrome infant in East Rutherford that 80 miles away in West Springfield there is a splendid assessment centre which connects effectively with the various services.

Let us be fair. We understand there is a fixed beginning service for this mother, and that is the visit from the District Nurse which the mother of the new born handicapped infant would get at home if she leaves the hospital within 10 days after delivery. The District Nurse presumably would alert the Health Visitor, and indeed many of the services needed, some of which I have outlined earlier, could well be provided by a Health Visitor, such as assistance in feeding the child. Less clear is from which source the Health Visitor would get consultation with a more complicated problem a mother encounters in feeding her child, one that calls for consultation with a nutritionist. And what about some of the other areas where the family of the handicapped child needs help, problems that relate not so much to physical factors as to his or her general growth in terms of speech development, sensory and motor training, and early cognitive responses? This does not seem to be an area in which Health Visitors are trained, nor is it something that has been covered by the conventional training of the social worker in the local social service department. And how about educators? They seem to be tied to the classroom or in any case (because there are domiciliary teachers) to the school curriculum, which does not include this type of consideration.

It seems then that the relatively simple array of services which constitute a program of early intervention are not at the moment in the competence of the front line workers in the local departments of health, education, or social service. This then is a problem that urgently calls for remedial action. However, we do not believe that it calls so much for a new "caring profession," as has been suggested, but rather for a reorientation in the training of health visitors and social workers. At the moment, educators seem rather far removed from this area, but we strongly agree with Barbara Tizard's recent statement in the Times Educational Supplement, in which she made an eloquent case for the need for nursery school education (Tizard, 1975). Once we get properly trained staff for this type of activity into the local education departments, we will have the kind of staff that will be able to assist parents.

And this brings me to the final challenge I want to point out to you, and as so often in the human services field it is a problem of communication. Let me bring it so you in the words of a Health Visitor:

> The health visitor must be ready to spend time and imagination so the parents of the handicapped know what services are available, where they are, and how to obtain them. She must be able to refer children to the appropriate agencies and be aware not only of the statutory provisions, but of the help that voluntary societies can offer. The needs of handicapped children are met by workers from various disciplines. There is a great need for each of us to repose confidence in the professional skills of others and therefore it should be possible to

exchange all available information about the families we are trying to help with colleagues in other fields. Too often a wrong concept of "confidentiality" prevents health visitors receiving information about treatment advised by experts and given to the families of handicapped children. Surely this is unacceptable if the health is to give the support the mother needs, and if she is to help the family to carry out the advised procedure correctly. (Byrne, 1971)

It seems to me this is a good point from which to start our discussion.

Chapter 5

An International Look
at Developmental Disabilities*

I think it is fair to say that the two mainsprings in the introduction of the developmental disabilities legislation in our country were, on the one hand, the recognition that combining the interests of several disability groups might provide greater political clout, and, on the other hand, the recognition that groups originally selected under this designation had the following in common: the particular needs related to management of disability in the early years of child development, and the dearth of services available to meet these needs. Early intervention, not just limited to early diagnosis but effective help to the home to assist the family in meeting the needs of the infant and very young child with severe handicap, has been almost universally neglected, as my husband and I have found in consultation visits to some 35 countries.

The reasons for this neglect doubtless vary from country to country. There is, for instance, the cultural tradition that very young children should be the responsibility of their mother, and there is the bureaucratic problem of delivering services to the home. Another factor may well have been that the parents, who in the 1950s and 1960s themselves organized cooperative services for their handicapped children and through their Associations demanded help from the State, mostly had children of school age or older.

To be sure, in some countries counseling was offered to parents to help them deal with their "psychological problems," but what disturbs parents in the first place is the frustration of not knowing

---

* University of California Extension, Berkeley, California, 1979

how to help their child effectively, and about such practical matters the counselors had little to say. Increasingly, countries developed clinics which provided diagnostic services, but these too rarely offered the kind of practical advice which could be utilized by parents at home.

While there are some notable exceptions, on the whole it can be said for all the countries that when these severely handicapped children are admitted to an educational program (and there are marked differences in the age of admission), their level of functioning—and their resulting disablement—is distinctly below what could have been possible in view of the original impairment. This may refer to speech and other means of communication, nourishment and eating habits, toileting, and the whole range of sensory-motor activities and social adaptations which are of such crucial significance in the development of a severely handicapped child. In addition, there are specific health problems such as the correction of orthopedic, visual, and hearing defects which often remain unattended to the detriment of the child's developmental potential. Last, but by no means least, should be mentioned a frequently encountered unduly low level of physical activity. Traditional overprotectiveness keeps parents (and others) from encouraging the child to engage in active physical exercises (walking, running, jumping, ball playing), and this is reinforced by a low level of expectancy in this regard, which most likely was conveyed to parents in their contacts with professional workers.

In short, granted that there are notable exceptions, it can be said that in most cases, developmentally disabled infants and very young children and their families face an unavailability of the most essential services and a disregard of the most self-evident needs in the most natural setting, the family home.

A British pediatrician, Frederic Brimblecombe, well known for his imaginative approach to early intervention with handicapped children, has described his recognition of this service void and his response to it as follows:

> In Exeter, we made a survey of the unmet needs of handicapped children and their families. Our study was controlled (in the scientific sense) in that for each family with a handicapped child we interviewed

a similar family without a handicapped child. In all, from a birth population of 6,000 children we found 310 children who had had a significant handicap identified before their 5th birthday (and 310 families without handicapped children who had a child of the same age, of the same family size and the same socioeconomic class). The "control" families had in many respects as many unmet needs as the handicapped families. When these had been equated we identified three particular unmet needs of the group who had handicapped children. These can be summarized.

1. A need for more information about the nature of the child's handicap.

2. A wish by the family to be helped to become more self-reliant in dealing with the child's handicap; in other words a failure by the professionals to transfer to the parents the special skills, confidence and courage needed to help their child achieve this full potential.

3. A need for more family support. The families with a handicapped child felt themselves to be isolated, the brothers and sisters deprived of many social facilities, a high risk of marriage breakdown among the parents, and above all a gradual erosion of their courage and strength so that at last exhausted and bitterly humiliated by their failure to cope, a number of families had sought institutional care for their handicapped child. (Brimblecombe, 1978)

These findings caused Dr. Brimblecombe and his associates to ask some searching questions about the usefulness of the services then being offered to such families, and also to inquire into the adequacy of those who render these services, as well as the appropriateness of their professional training. He continues in his report as follows:

The answers to these questions were not reassuring. The services provided clearly failed in many respects to meet the expressed needs of families with handicapped children. It was decided to experiment by providing a different type of resource aimed to achieve [the following:]

1. "More than words and talk; it must be genuine and show itself in action." Only in this way could the relationship between the family and the professional begin to measure up to what we sought to achieve.

2. A service which enabled families to achieve the skills, self-reliance and confidence:
    a) To provide for their own needs
    b) To assist them to know what services to seek and obtain when faced with problems beyond their own capabilities. (Brimble-combe, 1978)

Certainly this points up very forcefully the broad opportunities social workers have to participate in a program of early intervention alongside a broad array of such other specialists as pediatricians, developmental psychologists, teachers, nurses, and the practitioners in occupational, speech, and physiotherapies. Again I quote from Dr. Brimblecombe's report:

> From the start, one member of the center became the named person who would be responsible for ensuring that the needs of that particular family were met. This person irrespective of his discipline would be responsible for ensuring that the three main aims of our project were achieved for the particular family: (1) that the family fully understood the nature of their child's handicap; (2) that they were enabled to learn the skills and achieve the confidence to help their child achieve his full potential; (3) that they received all the family support that they needed. Once the total needs of the child have been identified, a treatment plan is made in full discussion with the parents and also with the single member of staff (irrespective of discipline) who will work directly with them. From then on, the treatment is carried out at home by the parents supported by regular home visits by the member of staff responsible. Where problems arise the particular member of staff and the parents can at any time obtain expert advice from the particular professional in whose discipline the difficulty lies. At the same time, a close relationship develops between the member of staff and the family. The family is provided with a confidante who will at all times be available when needed.
>
> In addition the Center itself is available for family support. It is open every day and night throughout the year. The child can come whenever the parents wish and for periods which they themselves select, for the day, for the night, for weekends or for longer periods depending upon the needs. Most parents decide to have a regular arrangement so that they know in advance that their child will spend two regular days a week at the Center or alternate weekends. They also know that they can call upon us for help at any time in an emergency . . . No one wears uniforms; the atmosphere is informal. Children and

parents come and go, both for a day and for short term residential care as their own family needs require. Parents are key members of the policy committee which has been formed to decide further developments in the service. (Brimblecombe, 1978)

Let me re-emphasize: this brief account of Dr. Brimblecombe's work in Devon is presented here as a shining example of what ought to but generally does not yet exist in England.

Marked exceptions to the general neglect of the earliest years of the child with developmental disabilities exist elsewhere as well, some of them, of course, in California. Indeed, it was our close acquaintance with the Developmental Center at the Children's Hospital of Los Angeles which first directed my husband's and my attention to the importance of early intervention.

The Retarded Infant Services in New York City pioneered in the early 1960s and the United Cerebral Palsy Associations maintained at about the same time some striking demonstration programs of work with families on behalf of children multiply handicapped to a most severe degree. The American Academy of Pediatrics in recent years has begun to push early screening programs to discover children with handicaps at the earliest possible age. But in New Zealand such a nationwide screening program has been going on for at least twenty years through a cooperative scheme of public and private resources.

South America, overall, is extremely backward in social services in general and services to developmentally disabled children in particular. Yet 15 years ago, in Montevideo, Uruguay, Eloisa de Lorenzo, an educator and psychologist, persuaded the University Hospital to start a program of early intervention for high risk children, with a strong research component. At about the same time, over in Buenos Aires we visited the clinic of Lydia de Coriat, a neurologist, and saw her developmental program for infants with Down's syndrome and for those having neurological disorders, a program with strong parent participation which was years ahead of what could be found in most university hospitals in our country at the time. A key member of Dr. Coriat's team was an early childhood educator who worked with parents and their infants both at the clinic and in their homes.

These few examples must suffice to make the point that the shopworn phrase "islands of excellence" is most appropriate in this context, because even in their own country these islands of excellence often remain unconnected to the "mainland of practice." There is for instance a service known as a toy library and consultation center initiated in Sweden by Karen Stensland Junker in the early 1960s. (Her book about her autistic daughter Boel, *The Child in the Glass Ball*, was published in English in 1964.) Toy libraries are easily set up and can be run most economically—e.g., one day a week, on Saturday, after school hours, using the school building, a private home, or the public library. It is a service which can bring to parents both reassurance and stimulation in a non-threatening, appealing setting, and can be of great benefit to the child. Yet, until very recently, this significant component of an early intervention program which has been repeatedly reported in the literature was found in any quantity only in Sweden, Norway, Great Britain, and Australia. By the way, a good Parent/Child Toy Lending Library how-to-manual was already produced here in Berkeley by the Far West Laboratory for Educational Research and Development in 1972. I hope that at least some in this audience have seen this manual and recognized its usefulness in work with families of developmentally disabled children as well as with the non-handicapped children for whom it was prepared.

A vital aspect of the developmental disabilities legislation and its underlying philosophy is the participation of disabled persons and their families in planning and decision making processes. In our country this has been laid down in rather elaborate fashion, both in the statute and in regulations, not only in developmental disabilities law but also in the Rehabilitation Act in general, and in the Education for All Handicapped Children Act of 1975—Public Law 94-142. Other countries have not developed as elaborate and detailed a statutory approach in this regard, but the principle of greater participation of the handicapped person and his or her family is very much in evidence.

As a matter of fact, already in 1971 the International League of Societies for the Mentally Handicapped held a Symposium on Cooperation between Parents, Clients, and Staff, attended by delegates from 13 countries. One section of the conclusions of this symposium dealt with obstacles on the way to the desired cooperation and their possible solution. This was presented in three segments, one dealing with the parents, one with the personnel, and one with the handicapped people themselves. Since our Conference today deals with the functioning of social workers in the field of developmental disabilities, let me read to you the paragraph concerned with personnel:

> The problem for the personnel is that it is difficult for the professionals to accept parents as equal partners in the team. Even so the personnel often feel that parents are too emotionally involved.
>
> The personnel often do not understand the emotional involvement of the parents as a natural and understandable phenomenon and are not able to understand that parents also must go through a certain development.
>
> Insufficient education in many disciplines is a reason for too little knowledge about families with handicapped children. Therefore specific and practical advice and assistance is often needed. (ILSMH, 1971)

Much of this advice has come to professional workers from experienced leaders in the parent movement. Particularly in the Scandinavian countries there developed an attitude of mutual respect between the professional workers and administrators and the parent activists, a respect which permitted much joint planning and joint decision making.

While programs initiated by the parents were gradually given over to the public agencies, this has not been the case with one program area, parent-to-parent counseling. In both Norway and Sweden this activity of the associations is financially supported by the government. In France there developed a nationwide program known as Action Interfamiliale—Interfamily Action,—which uses experienced parents to help "new" families and those who have difficulties coping with their handicapped child. Indeed, in France and some other countries there is a distinct trend which goes beyond parent-to-parent counseling to family-to-family interaction, an interesting parallel to family oriented counseling, which is increasingly used by social agencies in this country. Worth noting is a development in Metropolitan Toronto where the interfamilial action, "Extend-a-Family," is neighborhood based and included families with and without a handicapped child.

Significant as is the parent participation in planning and decision making and in counseling, of even greater significance in terms of policy development will be, in the long run, the participation of the persons with developmental disabilities themselves. Exciting things are already happening in this respect in a number of countries. Sweden took the lead, followed by England, Canada, France, and the United States. Tomorrow, an organization of developmentally disabled persons known as PEOPLE FIRST is holding a two-day conference in San Francisco, its first in the Bay Area.

The problem one encounters is twofold. On the one hand, many disabled people have never had a chance to learn how to make a decision; further, both parents and professional workers have been so convinced that the handicapped person is unable to make decisions that they are apt to hinder rather than further such attempts. Yet progress is being made everywhere. If only time would permit, I could tell you about a group of persons with cerebral palsy, confined—quite inappropriately—in an institution for the retarded, who managed to appear before a legislative committee pleading for funds so they could move into the community. I could tell you about a group of severely, multiply handicapped men with epilepsy who, after long years in an institution, are now living in a community group home, without house staff, largely managing their own affairs. I could tell you about the succinct criticism a group of Swedish developmentally disabled young people brought forth regarding many aspects of their programs as planned by a benevolent, sympathetic administration.

One of the main features of our revised developmental disabilities legislation is a Protection and Advocacy system. Here, too, other countries have not developed as formal a program as we have, but advocacy and the related activity of monitoring are significant features in many countries.

In Norway each county has a monitoring team of 6 persons, two of whom are to be selected by the parent associations; the British Spastics Society has been an outstanding, effective monitor of governmental action; and the Dutch Cerebral Palsy Society, several years ago spun off all direct services in order to give its full attention to advocacy and monitoring.

In this area too there is now direct involvement of the handicapped people themselves. In Denmark, for instance, by government regulation every facility serving handicapped persons must arrange monthly meetings to give the clients an opportunity to register complaints, ask questions, make suggestions. Minutes must be kept and must indicate how matters were followed up.

To some of you the matters I have presented may appear unduly optimistic if not altogether unrealistic. What needs to be stressed is that in education, and in rehabilitation, we are now making progress even with the most severely multiply handicapped individuals.

And one further comment needs to be made. So many of our past views were based on the performance of severely disabled persons who had not received proper medical attention, and not even minimal schooling or socializing experiences. It is obviously totally inappropriate to make our projection into the future based on the results of unjustified deprivations of the past.

In focusing on our topic today, Developmental Disabilities, I have had to draw of necessity on examples from countries whose perception of these problems and whose practical approaches are fairly similar to ours in the USA. I would not want to leave you with the impression that there is little going on in countries such as Spain, where the International Cerebral Palsy Society will be meeting in June, or Egypt, where the government has an active concern in adolescents with mental retardation and cerebral palsy — adolescents so often left out of rehabilitation schemes. In Africa, Christine Kenyatta, daughter of Kenya's late President, has focused attention on the whole area of special education. Ghana's voluntary association for the mentally handicapped began its work by establishing in 1970 a home for severely handicapped children who had been vegetating in a mental hospital. In the large cities we have visited in Brazil we saw good medical rehabilitation facilities for children with cerebral palsy and with epilepsy.

For those of you interested in a broad gauged approach to rehabilitation there are interesting developments to report from countries such as France, Germany, Sweden, and Australia, which have strong, government supported coordinating councils involving all the disabilities.

Further and finally, the topic as formulated did not give me a chance to report on the great contributions made by the United Nations, its Specialized Agencies such as the World Health Organization, UNESCO, the International Labor Organization, and, last but not least, the work of the international voluntary organizations which have banded together in the Council of World Organizations Interested in the Handicapped, known as CWOIH.

This is the International Year of the Child, proclaimed by the United Nations and promoted by UNICEF through all UN member governments. 1981 has been proclaimed the International Year for Disabled Persons, promotion being organized through UN's Division of Social Affairs, so I sincerely hope there will be opportunities for you to become acquainted with the broad range of the international agencies and their work, and their hopes for a world which recognizes that "it is normal to be different."

Chapter 6
The Needs of Children*

It is very appropriate that the International League of Societies for the Mentally Handicapped celebrates the twentieth anniversary of the United Nations Declaration of the Rights of the Child with a Symposium entitled, "The Mentally Retarded Child Today—The Adult of Tomorrow." At the time that this United Nations Declaration was adopted, there was still a widespread belief that children with mental retardation remained children all their lives, were children who "never grew." They were, as the title of a widely acclaimed Canadian film indicated, "Eternal Children." Like its predecessor, the Universal Declaration of Human Rights, the Declaration of the Rights of the Child basically emphasized the dignity inherent in the human existence, and for children, this dignity rests in our respect for their potential to become adults, their growth into adulthood.

There has been a very significant change in this regard on a broad international scale, and the large number of national member associations of the International League who do not have or have removed the word *children* from their name furnishes just one indication of this change. But the title for our Symposium, "The Mentally Retarded Child Today—The Adult of Tomorrow," goes farther. It obviously proclaims that the child, today still characterized and stereotyped as retarded, may tomorrow be just an adult. Does this mean "one of us" and no longer "one of them"?

What are the chances that this goal might be reached? What are the impediments we must recognize and neutralize or combat? Obviously the first factor we must deal with is that of health. To become a healthy adult a child should be born in a healthy

---

* Symposium of ILSMH, San Juan, Puerto Rico, 1979.

environment to a healthy mother and get adequate nourishment and care during the early years. In industrial countries, very considerable progress has been made during the past twenty years in prenatal services, in attendance at birth, and in services to the baby and mother. Infant mortality and morbidity rates are closely watched by governments in these countries, and there is almost a competitive spirit to push progress ahead of neighboring countries. Special protection during pregnancy, free checkups on the newborn, and documentation such as the Austrian Mutter/Kind Pass (a health passport for mother and child) are offered with increasing frequency.

But the situation is radically different in many of the developing countries. Far from having even marginal health care facilities and services, they cannot even assure the first requirement for survival, a minimum of nutrition. Maternal malnutrition to the extreme degree that is widespread in the world's poorest countries has been shown to be a significant contributing factor—directly and indirectly—to mental retardation in the newborn. Obviously, of equal significance is a minimum adequate nutrition for the infant during the early years of fastest growth. FAO, the Food and Agricultural Organization in the UN family, is indeed, in developing areas of the world, a major rehabilitation agency, with its mission to increase production of foodstuff and to work toward efficient and equitable distribution and transportation of available supplies.

Parallel with FAO's efforts is the work of UNICEF, which technically is no longer called an Emergency Fund but whose work in arranging mass feeding for children certainly is and for a long time will continue to be of emergency nature. Added to this are the activities of the World Health Organization in the field of maternal and child health, epidemiology, and disease control.

But what else needs to be done in countries whose children suffer extreme deprivation? A colleague of ours recently travelled to India to get a first hand experience of the mental retardation situation there and if possible offer some help. A letter from him has this to say:

As you know quite well, the poverty is so severe in India that it is difficult knowing where to start. All efforts being done to help the poor are just scratching the surface of the known need . . . Mother Teresa's homes have several hundred retarded children and some adults, but no education is being provided, only maintenance . . . They primarily see their role as one where they provide T.L.C. and not training and not education . . . When the basic needs of food, shelter, and clothing are not being provided for so many millions, it would be difficult to spend limited resources on training handicapped persons. In India they must spend their time on issues relating to life, before they can address the issue of the quality of life.

I am not surprised about his reaction because it is shared by many of our colleagues. However, there are some considerations that should be further pursued during our discussions. In the first place, while it is, of course, true that in India people are starving and are without minimum shelter, there are also cities like Bombay, Bangladore, and Delhi, where large numbers of people live in comfort and have university educations. If they have a handicapped child with blindness or mental retardation, they, like similarly situated parents elsewhere in the world, want their child to have health and educational services. Indeed, there are more than one hundred specialized programs for retarded children and adults in India. How can this all be reconciled?

In the areas of extreme deprivation, handicapped children should be served along with all other children in the mass programs in nutrition, health, and sanitation—they should not be excluded from such programs merely because of their handicap. Obviously the actual delivery of specialized services for handicapped children in these deprived areas, be they in health or in education, will have to wait, but what is essential is that those charged with the planning and development of education, health, and welfare services for the general population must be aware that, as conditions improve, an increasing number of handicapped children will have to be served, and that it will be more costly and in the long run far less effective to have services develop as a separate, segregated system. In the meantime the services being developed in the cities will fulfill an important function: They can serve as demonstration projects to develop appropriate practices, *indigenous to the country*, as teaching laboratories and study centers, providing knowledge which can later be applied in the more deprived areas.

There are two factors that need to be stressed in thinking about initiation of services for handicapped children. The first is that long before a country of limited means can establish a full service pattern, significant work can be done on a simplified and partial basis. A fully equipped screening mechanism reaching all children ages one, two, and four will for most developing countries be a far distant goal, but good deployment of public health nurses will permit a good bit of partial or pre-screening, and indeed parents can be instructed to watch for certain indicators of trouble ahead, and, when they occur, communicate with the public health nurse or a similar health resource.

UNICEF, in similar fashion, has undertaken in several countries a nutritional program teaching parents good diet ideas for small children, and better utilization of local food resources. Obviously, member associations of the League can be of considerable assistance in such a program. A good example of opportunity for effective parent education would be combating the kind of specific and tragic problem created in developing countries by the promotion (by Nestle or other companies) of dried milk products to the exclusion of breast feeding, although it is not always easy to have a somber warning about probable damage and death compete with the colorful enticement of the commercial corporation.

During this Year of the Child there has been in many aspects a renewed emphasis on the role of the family, both in the area of prevention and early intervention. In many ways, parents can be helped to work with the pre-school handicapped child, avoiding the pitfalls which have occurred in the well-to-do industrialized countries, where for some quite inexplicable reason early intervention was generally neglected until the recent past, and where organized programs started with school age or a bit later. The practical aspect of this is that much of the work in early intervention (avoidance of overprotection, exposure to stimulating experiences, speech encouragement, socializing contacts with other children and with adults) can in most instances be arranged with very modest expense and yet great effectiveness, as compared with the maintenance of large institutions, extensive testing programs, or routine comprehensive diagnostic studies.

Quite obviously here is an opportunity for the League's member societies to demonstrate such services on a limited basis and to push for their adoption by their government, while the League's Secretariat, supported by a relevant Committee, should pursue this matter on the United Nations level.

PART III

Issues in
Special Education

Chapter 7

Meeting Special
Educational Needs*

Special education has seen an unprecedented growth in the 1960s and 1970s. There are many reasons for this, and different countries might not agree about their relative importance. Most prominent was the development of a much more positive attitude toward disabled children and their capacity to learn. This was undoubtedly at least in part the consequence of the astonishing progress made during and after World War II in the field of rehabilitation, as much with regard to physical as to mental disabilities. Some of it developed along with a fundamental shift in the field of education: where once there had been quite separated programmes of schooling for the various handicaps, there was a growing recognition of basic concepts and approaches underlying the schooling for children with all these various disabilities. In short, special education developed as a unified field, with new knowledge, new skills, and new and innovative teaching methods. Without doubt, one of the most significant attitude changes, beginning in the mid-1960s, was acceptance of the concept that "No Child is Ineducable," regardless of degree of handicap (Segal, 1967).

The first international policy statement in support of special education programs emanated not from an educational source but from the International Labor Organization (ILO). In 1955 the International Labor Conference passed Recommendation 99 Concerning Vocational Rehabilitation of the Disabled. Section IX deals with special provisions for disabled children and young persons and states that "educational programmes should take into

---

* This is a composite of presentations made in Chicago, 1970, in Brazzaville, Kongo, in 1980, and in San Juan, Puerto Rico, in 1985.

account the special problems of disabled children and young persons to receive educational and vocational preparation best suited to their age, abilities, aptitudes and interests." Moreover, this Section calls for integration by stating that such education "should be developed within the general framework of such services to non-disabled children and young persons, and should be conducted, wherever possible and desirable, under the same conditions as, and in company with non-disabled children and young persons."

At the time ILO passed this surprisingly progressive recommendation, the field of education had no international organizational body dealing with the educational needs of disabled children and young people. Significantly, it was the International Society for the Rehabilitation of the Disabled, today known as Rehabilitation International, which recognized the need for international exchange of ideas and practices in this area, setting up a standing commission on special education which since 1960 has held seminars in conjunction with its world congresses on rehabilitation.

To underline the significance of the initiative taken by ILO on behalf of special education, it should be mentioned that when the United Nations passed the Declaration of the Rights of the Child in 1959, it merely provided that "the child who is physically, mentally or socially handicapped shall be given the special treatment, education and care required by the particular condition," without any reference to integration or even the need to develop such services within the general framework of education.

But where was UNESCO, the United Nations Educational, Scientific and Cultural Organization, founded in 1946 with the aim of promoting collaboration among nations in the fields of education, science, and culture? It was not until 1964, nine years after ILO's Recommendation 99, that several Scandinavian countries introduced to UNESCO's delegate body a resolution for the establishment of a special education program within UNESCO. And it was not until 1968 that Niels-Ivar Sundberg was placed in charge of this program.

The establishment of this special education office within

UNESCO had a very considerable effect. On the one hand, it gave this area greater worldwide visibility and a base for broader action, and on the other hand it helped initiate an international network of communication, exchange, and collaboration. UNESCO's role in that was especially important because, notwithstanding widespread activities in the education of disabled pupils in selected countries around the world, there had not developed an international organization of special educators and only a few such associations existed on a national or regional level.

Perhaps the most significant event was an Expert Meeting on special education convened at UNESCO headquarters in Paris in December 1968 with specialists from ten countries. The following excerpts from the official report of this meeting will provide you a flavor of the thinking of the group, which included educators from India, the United Arab Republic, Uruguay, and the USSR:

> All countries in the world need to develop and improve their provisions for special education. The need is urgent. All existing efforts are therefore to be encouraged, without waiting for the achievement of ideal plans or programmes . . . The starting point is to clarify the place of special education in the general national system of education. In fact, special education is a branch or offshoot of general education, and should, like general education, be directed to the integration of the individual in society . . .
>
> Only by means of competent and qualified leaders in both the central and local administration is it possible to secure a proper education for the handicapped . . .
>
> National policies in regard to special education should be directed to the goals of providing equal access for all to education and of integrating all citizens into the economic and social life of the community. . . . The aims of special education for those who show mental, sensorial, physical or emotional impediments are precisely those of education in general, i.e., offering the child the maximum opportunity to develop cognitive, scholastic and social skills to the highest possible level . . .
>
> We know that for administrative reasons it was and is sometimes necessary to segregate children according to a dominant characteristic, but the cause of a child's learning difficulty frequently is unknown and a child may have more symptoms than the one used to label him. When an ordinary education programme is unaware of these problems, the

child may be seen as an unapproachable problem and therefore never receive treatment, or receive one according to the category in which he is placed. This labelling and segregation of a child from the assistance of educational programmes tends to place emphasis on the deficit, so he is often treated as "mentally retarded, blind, emotionally disturbed," and many other characteristics that will contribute in his future may not be taken into account. It is the whole child that has to be considered by the educator, never a part of the child . . .

Special education services must rest on the right of every individual to be a part of and not apart from society and must be placed in the context of a realistic appraisal of the needs and possibilities of the community in which he lives . . .

The role of special education lies in the early identification and treatment of the problem, as well as provision for an adequate integration of services. Special education must break away from the stagnation implied by the words *special, bias, different and segregated*. Its philosophy should be formulated so as to maintain its identity in the framework of ordinary education. (UNESCO, 1969)

Since the general purpose of this advisory meeting was to make recommendations regarding the broad outlines of a long term UNESCO special education program, the group's nine recommendations are of particular interest. It is not possible to comment on all, but the following should be noted:

The establishment of special education services, it must be emphasized, is important and urgent. It would seem that the development of special education can be facilitated by including it within the general educational system where it can take advantage of the existing educational infrastructure and services.

This redirection with a community slant, and the integration of special education in general educational services in the various countries imply that UNESCO's special education programmes should likewise be integrated in its general educational programmes, and that policy in the various Education Sector services (planning, teacher training, adult education) should follow suit accordingly.

In planning activities, the priority accorded a particular category of handicap should reflect the specific circumstances and needs of the country concerned. In general, however, the education of mental defectives deserves special attention; they constitute the largest category and their education is usually the least developed, quantitatively and qualitatively.

And finally,

> UNESCO should undertake to inform the public of the problems and needs, especially the economic aspects of educating the handicapped so that they can take a full share in the active life of the community. Since the parents and families of handicapped children have often initiated the demand for, and the provision of, services in special education, principally by setting up local and national associations, UNESCO should seek co-operation with such associations through their parent organizations or co-ordinating bodies. (UNESCO, 1969)

The quality of this document, prepared by specialists from ten countries in different parts of the world, underlines the great potential that lies in such international collaboration.

Once Mr. Sundberg assumed his duties, things began to happen, and within a few years UNESCO indeed had become the major international resource in all aspects of special education. His untimely death in November 1981 while he was attending in Madrid the World Conference on Actions and Strategies for Education, Prevention, and Integration was a tremendous loss to the international community and particularly to children in need of special educational services. In appreciation of his invaluable work, the conference brought together its recommendations and resolutions in a document they entitled the "Sundberg Declaration." (Available from the Special Education Unit, UNESCO, Place de Fontenoy in Paris.)

There is one specific aspect of Mr. Sundberg's work that I would like to mention. Almost all the special education studies done under UNESCO auspices during his tenure included information on both developed and developing countries, side by side. A volume entitled *Case Studies in Special Education* (1974) dealt with Cuba, Japan, Kenya, and Sweden; *Integration of Technical and Vocational Education into Special Education* (1980) included Austria, Colombia, Iran, and Tunisia, while *Handicapped Children: Early Detection, Intervention and Education* (1980) had selected case studies from as wide an array as Argentina, Canada, Denmark, Jamaica, Jordan, Nigeria, Sri Lanka, Thailand, and the United Kingdom. Along with those outstanding publications, UNESCO has also organized and published reports on regional and subregional seminars full of vital information for practitioners and administrators alike.

My frequent reference to developing and developed countries needs some qualification. It obviously is not possible to speak of developing countries as if they constituted a group with similar characteristics. Just as one can observe in industrialized countries wide variations in special education policy and even more so in special education practices (e.g., between Italy, Spain, England, and the USA), so too can one observe wide differences between nations of Africa or Asia. Furthermore, particularly in developing countries there are radical differences between larger industrialized cities and the vast rural areas, where the overriding concerns deal with the need for water, food, and the most basic sanitation and health care. In the past, this has led some experts to feel that even to mention special education services in such countries is nonsensical. Such a view is obviously short-sighted. One must plan ahead for the day when these more basic human needs are increasingly met. This was brought home to me in the mid-1960s when my husband and I received a call for help from a public health pediatrician in a West African country. As they had been able over a period of years to improve maternal and child health care in their city, they found themselves faced by a growing number of young children with severe impairment. Formerly these babies would have died early, but now they survived into school age; yet, as far as the school authorities were concerned, there were no educational provisions whatsoever. Initially the pediatrician and her staff had tried to meet the developmental needs of these children by improvised activities, but the problem was growing beyond their capacity and resources.

On looking at the many and pervasive changes which have occurred in the last two decades of a developing country which is in the process of long range planning for the education of *all* its children, including those who are handicapped, one might well consider integration the key concept, and the basis for a number of crucial policy determinations.

In the first place, it is important that special education in all its aspects should be administered as a part of general education, and the training of special education teachers should proceed within the overall framework of teacher education.

To understand the extent to which special education in various countries has been administered as a separate entity and in various instances even as part of the Ministry of Welfare, or the Ministry of Health, rather than the Ministry of Education, one must be mindful that to a considerable extent special education got its original impetus and guidance from the field of medicine. It was the physicians who recognized the educational potential as well as the special educational needs of their child patients, and terms like "Heilerziehung," "curative education," and "institut medico-pedagogique" remind us of this.

There is no need to discuss in detail the historical developments which increasingly have brought special education closer to general education. The establishment by UNESCO of its program in special education bears testimony to that. But it is important to remember that already in 1965 the late Professor Jack Tizard, great social psychologist and pioneer in the field of mental retardation, pointed out in England that the next major advancement in special education had to come from the field of general education. For him it was of the essence that the general classroom teacher gain a better knowledge and understanding of the nature and variety of human growth and behaviour; that the general teacher be more accepting of differences and more understanding and knowledgeable of the work of his or her colleagues in special education (Tizard, 1965).

However, in some industrialized countries one can observe even today a big and at times acrimonious struggle when efforts are underway to make special education a real part of general education. There is as much resistance on the part of general education to welcome the children with special needs and their teachers as there is resistance on the other side to give up what is seen as the advantage of a separate and specialized existence. That this is a matter of continuing concern is attested by the fact that as late as 1970 an African country considered establishing a department of labour, welfare, and youth that would be responsible for special education, rather than placing it within the department of education (UNESCO, 1971).

On the other hand, countries which in the past provided schooling for the more severely handicapped children under the auspices of Ministries of Health or of Social Welfare (Great Britain and Denmark, for example) have now made these school programs the responsibility of the Education Authorities. The 1979 UNESCO Expert Meeting on Special Education emphasized that even the most severely handicapped child should be included. Specifically, the meeting urged that

> when a new mandatory law is introduced on compulsory education, this should include children with all ranges of disabilities, including the most severely handicapped. Where compulsory laws exist, the Ministry of Education should not disclaim the responsibility for certain categories of handicapped children. Experience has demonstrated that special education programmes enrich the education offerings for all children. (UNESCO, 1979a)

It might be noted that accounts of programs for severely and profoundly handicapped children located in a regular school often point out that non-handicapped children vie for a chance to assist the children in these special classes, accepting them and their disabilities without prejudice.

Integration as opposed to segregation should be seen in this context. What happened in many countries where there was an early development of special education services was that these schools or centers grew up as quite separate and apart from the general education schools and services, with the result that, later on, elaborate, at times expensive, and in any case complex and time consuming steps had to be taken toward a rapprochement. Every effort should therefore be made in countries which have not yet developed a general school system to avoid segregation measures in the first place.

We have here a parallel to the concept of *normalization,* which N.E. Bank-Mikkelsen of Denmark (its first proponent) describes as being essentially an "anti-dogma," a move against "de-normalizing" patterns of life so frequently found in situations involving persons with mental retardation (Bank-Mikkelsen, 1980).

As Bank-Mikkelsen conceived the normalization principle, it is appropriate for any cultural situation. For example, eating patterns, meal times, sleeping quarters, and toilet customs may vary greatly between cultural regions, and what is normal in one may not be acceptable in another. Above all, normalization is not a rigid concept. Within any culture, differences exist, so that one can say *it is normal to be different.* Thus, although a person is different, it must be possible for him or her to live with others in an ordinary environment.

In the Report of the Regional Seminar on Education of Mentally Retarded Children in Asia and Oceania, held in 1978 in Australia and co-sponsored by UNESCO, one country reported the following:

> In our policy of education for the mentally retarded, we put special education in the normal system. Special education is a branch of normal education and this helps in the integration of the individual into society.

One of the recommendations at the close of the seminar was as follows:

Maximal integration of all mentally retarded persons into the general stream of education and the normal life of the community.

It was further agreed that the overriding policies for education of mentally retarded persons should be as follow:

> To educate them as closely as possible to the mainstream of educational services in ordinary classes, taking into account their special needs and the needs of other children.
> To prepare them to live as fully as possible as ordinary members of their adult community. (UNESCO, 1979b)

But it is not only with regard to general discrimination against persons with handicaps that the countries in early stages of development should beware of the example set by the industrialized countries. There is also the traditional separation between physical and mental handicap which promotes confusion and misunderstanding. Most individuals with a severe degree of mental handicap are multiply handicapped. Many have rather complex physical disabilities requiring attention, therapy, and correction.

In many cases their educational progress depends on treatment for and alleviation of their physical impairments. Yet, most unfortunately, they are often implicitly or explicitly excluded when programs for "physically handicapped" are planned.

Therefore it is noteworthy that tradition in Senegal "seems to ignore any rejection of handicapped people as well as any discrimination between different handicaps." That is why President Senghor, very conscious of the rapid change of traditional society in his country, would like to make permanent those attitudes of good will and acceptance now before they change. That is why he is planning services for handicapped persons through compulsory education, vocational training, and development of community help through the creation of volunteer associations (of parents) and volunteer work (UNESCO, 1979b).

At the same conference the President of the Mali Society for the Welfare of the Blind made particular reference to mentally handicapped people and their families when he insisted that attention must be drawn to *all* handicapped people.

These statements from African countries underline and reaffirm what the International League of Societies for the Mentally Handicapped emphasized in its submission of June 1979 to a UNESCO Consultation on Special Education:

> We feel it necessary to stress the need of mentally handicapped individuals because experience has repeatedly shown that their needs are either neglected or receive only secondary consideration within a wider framework of special education or rehabilitation. We therefore urge that any statement of special education policy made by UNESCO and other international organizations should make a direct and unambiguous reference to the effect that mentally handicapped people are explicitly included in the proposed special education policy.
>
> We make this suggestion because mentally handicapped people cannot easily speak for themselves, though we note with approval that they are now beginning to do so and that attempts are being made in certain countries to help them to express their own views about the quality of the services being provided for them. In general, however, mentally handicapped people have to rely on parents and professionals to act as spokesmen on their behalf. (ILSMH, 1979)

The principles are thus clearly laid down. The question is: how can they be realized? The UNESCO Expert Meeting on Special Education, held in Paris in October 1979, suggests appropriate action and direction:

> Early detection, assessment and intervention are indispensable prerequisites for successful integration of many handicapped children into regular schools, and can also enhance the developmental potential of many severely handicapped children, helping to prevent unwanted secondary problems. (UNESCO, 1979a)

The terms early detection and assessment should not be interpreted as meaning, of necessity, a full fledged "clinical" approach which obviously would not be feasible in countries lacking trained clinicians and also financial resources. Rather, this strategy (plan of action) is based on another factor—the recognition of the family as the greatest natural resource in the care and development of children with handicaps.

It is a common experience shared in most cultures that the birth of a child "who is different" brings not only grief to the family but also a disturbing uncertainty about how to meet the child's needs. Yet, increasingly, it has been recognized that particularly in the very early years the parents can be taught how to meet these needs, and many countries have developed such a service. One example of an effective program bringing help to parents of very young handicapped children at home is the Portage System, which has been successfully used in a number of countries. Its simple, basic approach of home teaching methods has general cross-cultural applicability.

Who could undertake the job of training parents to cope with their handicapped children and help them develop? This could and should be done by indigenous workers who in turn would be trained by a small team of professional persons. **

A word of caution is needed here: any approach that counts on collaboration with the family must make sure that all its commu-

---

** *The International League of Societies for the Mentally Handicapped recently submitted to the UN a proposal (for funding during the IYDP) for just such an early training project in order to develop systems of early intervention in some of the Asian countries.*

nications are written in a straight-forward, simple, and direct style. When the Frontier Society for the Mentally Handicapped in Peshawar, Pakistan, was preparing some material on home training of retarded children, they tried to make sure that all could understand, as parents, what the association was writing: "We involved all staff, the ayahs and van driver included. They have brought up seventeen children between them, and we made sure that our developmental details were relevant to their child rearing practices, and in language familiar to them" (Miles, 1980).

To be sure, even if written in simplest style, there are many areas of the world where only a minority of the parents can read such materials. For Pakistan, it would perhaps be 10 to 15 percent of ordinary parents. This suggests, of course, that parents be helped to share with other parents what they have learned (an important goal anywhere); it also suggests the use of pictures and posters and other aids. But from such simple beginnings there can develop a broader parent-to-parent (or family-to-family) program of assistance, a kind of community self-help, as has been demonstrated so effectively over the years by the French national parents' association UNAPEI.

Obviously, there are children who also need medical intervention—for example, to correct problems of vision, hearing, motricity, and mobility, in order to be prepared for a satisfactory school experience. It is of the essence that mentally handicapped children are not excluded from the basic child health services available in their country, as has happened in the past, and that any remedial treatment needed be started at the earliest possible time. A physical impairment is a burden to any child, but for mentally handicapped children in particular it accentuates their functional limitations and is likely to deprive them of essential developmental experiences.

Educational policies concerning mentally handicapped children even in the early 1960s contained many strange provisions, but perhaps the strangest was the one delaying their admission to special school programs. Since the children were "delayed," their school programs should be delayed—so went the rationalization. This myth was slow to die, but over the past decades, an increasing number of school programs have been providing for children as young as three years of age, and even in earliest infancy in certain conditions—blindness and deafness, for instance.

Altogether, there is an ever growing understanding that school readiness for severely retarded children is not a matter of waiting passively for them to arrive at some specific developmental point. Actually, the lack of stimulating developmental experiences has been found to result in quite unnecessary deterioration.

On the other hand, it is only realistic to recognize that the question of how soon children can be provided with a preschool program will depend on the particular country's economic situation.

An early intervention service in preparation for school admission which deserves special mention is the toy lending library and consultation service. Once again, here is a flexible service that can be adapted to a wide variety of cultural patterns and degrees of "industrialization." It is not expensive to run and does not require a special building. Children play in all societies, and their play constitutes a very important learning experience. Parents of a handicapped infant are apt to be so concerned about the "unknown" in their child's developmental problem that they overlook or shy away from the normal child rearing practices they used with their other children. However, for obvious reasons, developmentally handicapped children need more rather than less play experience. Toys help children learn to grasp objects, to hold them tight, to learn movement, and much more. Even though the "toys" might be only sticks or stones, parents can be taught ways to use them in play to improve the young child's motor control, for example. Even if the initial supply of toys available is no more than the simplest of objects, as the children grow older, they will use more sophisticated play things, and here the parents will benefit further from the consultation part of the service.

A toy library and consultation centre can be established with a minimal cost in the simplest quarters, open perhaps only one day a week; or it might be a traveling service brought to different towns and villages in an area. Children who have good play experience in the first years of life are more ready for preschool or some more informal, simpler group activity. This in turn will bring them ultimately to the school door vastly better prepared and far more acceptable to teachers (Farrell and Glue, 1978).

A forerunner to the toy library and consultation service was reaching families in rural areas of New Zealand already in the 1950s. From the Correspondence School section of the Department of Education in Wellington, the well known "green bags" with toys, play materials, and suggestions to parents were sent by free post to families with severely handicapped young children who lived too far away to attend a community school. The materials were exchanged every month or as needed, and were individually planned by a worker who knew the family and had visited the home, with personal contacts at least twice a year and regular communication by telephone and letters. Radio and television have also been used to provide such help to parents and children in isolated rural areas in a number of countries (Winterbourn, 1965).

Fortunately, there are far more preschool group experiences with handicapped and non-handicapped children together than have ever before been reported in the professional literature. More than 20 years ago, kindergartens in the State of South Australia had a policy of accepting up to three handicapped children in each group of twenty children, finding it a satisfying experience for all. Recently in Mauritius, as a follow-up to an internationally funded Joint Child Health and Education Project studying the effect of risk factors in young children, three "Pre-primary Integrated classes [were] established with 50 percent normal children and 50 percent handicapped and 'at risk' children"; this successful experiment will doubtless be a good stepping stone for development of a non-segregationist primary school system.

Much of the present hesitation toward (and in some cases open rejection of) a policy of integration in the schools is based on difficulties encountered in school systems (and communities in general) where children with handicaps have been segregated. Integration in the regular schools does by no means imply the absence of any special class, of special learning experience, in a so-called "resource room," for instance, where a child receives intensive speech training or remedial reading instruction. Such a policy, sometimes called "mainstreaming," does inveigh against special and separate schools or other arrangements which keep the children with handicaps from being together with non-handicapped children.

Thus in countries with traditional special education programs, "integration" is often seen as a controversial, new, intrusive concept, whereas in developing countries where segregational patterns have not yet been established, integration is more likely to be seen as a "normal" state of affairs.

Indonesia, with some traditional heritages of separate special education programs from its colonial days, is presently moving through an experimental period. A regional survey in Java, for instance, is investigating how far "mainstreaming" can be applied: a pilot project is integrating visually handicapped children in an ordinary elementary school. On North Sumatra, mentally retarded children of different ability levels are participating in a school program with physically handicapped children: "The learning environment in this program was carefully developed to put the child into a real life situation which invited him to be actively involved in tasks assigned to him. Individual attention is given to each to preserve his individuality while encouraging self expression and growth" (Semiawan, 1980).

Another pattern has developed in the Manila elementary school system, where overlarge special classes in local schools had become stigmatizing "dumping grounds," and where teachers felt alone and isolated. The solution found was to bring together these children into "centers" within a small number of regional elementary schools in the city, and to provide more adequate support services to the teachers, both in material resources as well as increased supervisory and consultation help. Re-integration of the children into regular classes of the school, full or part time, has been possible for many, particularly as they reach adolescence.

A few observations from other experiences of countries in early stages of development suggest some cautions: at times too much emphasis is placed on traditional psychological testing procedures imported from industrialized countries. Not only are they used without being adapted to the situation in the developing country, but in many cases these tests, their mode of application, and the classification schemes flowing from them are under question or outdated in the country of origin. An example is the sharp dichotomy between the so-called "educable" and "trainable" grouping.

Also, we categorize increasingly not by medical diagnosis but by the individual needs of the child (children with Down's syndrome are *not* all alike, nor is it helpful to call children with epilepsy "epileptics" or to speak of "autistics").

Significant differences of opinion have been evidenced between those who emphasize, as the most basic need, highly qualified staff *to carry out assessment* (with exclusion from school as a frequent result), and those who feel that priority should be given to *the teaching process.*

Finally, it needs to be said again: the great opportunity for developing countries, the great advantage they have over industrialized countries with long established, rigid school bureaucracies, lies in the opportunity to create a sound system from the ground up. Modest in its beginning stages because of the fiscal strictures and fiscal limitations, it can nevertheless be sound in design, in the foreknowledge that inevitably a growing number of children with increasingly more complex disabilities will need to be and can be well served in the regular school systems.

PART IV

Preparation for Adult Living

Chapter 8

Preparation of Persons with Mental Retardation for Adult Living*

Some time ago, Dr. Kan, the distinguished Japanese leader in mental retardation, prepared for an international congress in France a series of slides of new Japanese mental retardation institutions. In order to afford his western colleagues a more realistic opportunity to assess these institutional buildings, he started out with a number of slides showing typical Japanese middle-income and low-income housing as a basis for comparison.

I was reminded of this very thoughtful and very effective gesture when I began to think about what I wanted to say to you today, and realized how little I know about these, your Caribbean Islands, because this is indeed my first visit here.

Fortunately, I am aided by a new development in our field which evolves around the normalization principle, first formulated in the late 1960s by Bank-Mikkelsen of Denmark and Bengt Nirje of Sweden and very rapidly accepted in many countries as a guideline to programming. Most succinctly stated, the principle of normalization aims at making available to mentally retarded individuals patterns and conditions of everyday life which are as close as possible to the norms and patterns of the society of which they are a part. It goes without saying that such patterns and conditions vary according to age and differ as between city and rural areas; indeed, it is important in our context to be mindful of the fact that it is normal to be different. Thus, normalization does

* Third Caribbean Congress on Mental Retardation, Barbados, W.I., 1974.

not denote rigid patterns—to the contrary, in general, societal patterns make room for variations sufficiently to accommodate the major portion of mentally retarded adults. We have proof of this from the fact that in all countries where surveys of the prevalence of mental retardation are undertaken, we identify a large number of individuals as retarded in the school population, but the number identified in the adult population is distinctly smaller. In other words, many retarded individuals manage, once freed from the label of the special class, to melt into the general population, to adopt a lifestyle, however limited or marginal, which "gets by," which still falls within the flexible limits of what a community will accept. Most of us deviate in one way or another from accepted community norms, but that does not cause us to be called "deviants," as the sociologists use the term.

In any case, the principle of normalization makes it possible for me to present broad general outlines of new knowledge, new trends in the field of mental retardation which can be interpreted by you within your own societal frame of reference. There are two points which need to be underlined. Normalization does not imply that we "normalize" individuals. This would indeed have a very obnoxious connotation. Rather, it refers to the circumstances, the conditions, the rhythm of life. Furthermore, in the definition I gave before, the words "as close as possible" need to be emphasized, because this element of relativity makes it possible to apply this principle to even the most severely handicapped individuals. For them, too, we must see that provisions for their care do not deviate any more from what is commonly accepted in society than is specifically necessitated by their condition.

These introductory remarks may strike some of you as rather commonplace, as too self-evident to state them with such emphasis. Yet nothing has been more injurious to mentally retarded persons, nothing has handicapped them more than the preconceived notions, the prejudicial judgments with which they have been considered, and which, right to the present day, have constrained our programming.

The title for my presentation is "Preparing the Mentally Retarded for Adult Living." Yet some persons feel even today that mentally retarded individuals do not reach the status of adulthood. While we do not *hear* as much today about the "eternal child" as was the case some years ago, in many subtle and not so subtle ways the mentally retarded person is treated as if a child. In part this is reinforced by a very widespread misunderstanding of the psychologist's reference to mental age. Even in reputable psychological texts one still can read that a mental age of 9 means that the retarded adult can be expected to be like a child 9 years of age. Obviously, it would be rather futile, if this were true, to prepare such an individual for adult living. However, in the first place, a mental age of 9 signifies no more than that on one of the standard intelligence tests the overall performance of the person (i.e., his mental age) was arrived at by averaging out the individual's performance on numerous sub-tests, on some of which he or she may have scored as high as the 12 year level and on others below the 9 year level. Thus it is very misleading to liken that performance to that of a child of 9. In the second place, what is measured by the test is intellectual performance, a very partial assessment of a person that leaves out the capacity to adapt oneself to social situations, one's life experience, and the individual's degree of physical maturation, which allows for a greater range of activities than the 9 year old is capable of handling. All these factors make it possible for such a retarded person to assume adult roles which would be definitely closed to the 9 year old, and to perform adult tasks of which the 9 year old would be incapable, both physically and socially.

There was a time when it was at least excusable to think of mentally retarded persons just in terms of what was then familiar to us, the mentally retarded child seemingly incapable of achievement, appealing forever for our love and above all for our protection. And that protection was most easily effectuated by continuing to treat the mentally retarded as children, by relieving them (that was our reasoning) of the burden and danger connected with adult status.

There is no longer any excuse for this. The basic premises on which this point of view was based have been proven unfounded. Years of hard, imaginative pioneering by parents and professional workers have resulted in many cases in a complete reversal of what had once been accepted as definitive knowledge. Thus children once considered ineducable are today educated in the public schools. Retarded adults, once considered unemployable, are working in the competitive market. And others, once considered totally dependent and incapable of even self-care, not only have mastered those skills but leave the shelter of their home and are productively occupied in activity centers. Since I have been privileged to become acquainted with mental retardation facilities and services in some 35 countries, I can attest to the fact that demonstration projects incorporating this new knowledge are not just limited to a few advanced countries. They literally can be found around the globe. Yet tradition has great force—particularly so if it is linked to popular prejudice.

Thus, there has been considerable lag in the application of this new knowledge, both on the part of parents and on the part of professional persons. This latter point needs underlining. What is required is not just an effort to educate the parents and the general public with regard to the new dimensions of the problem of mental retardation; the professional practitioner, the college teachers, and the writers of textbooks used by the students need to be helped to shed old beliefs, and to recognize the faultiness of research studies previously accepted as definitive.

It is, of course, impossible to present to you a full account of all the new knowledge gained, and I must be content with a few examples. A good number of you are familiar with the fact that in the past it was generally believed that there was a group of individuals known as "profoundly retarded," of whom we accepted that they not only would never learn to dress themselves and to learn such elementary things as using the toilet, but we even accepted as a fact that once dressed they would not keep their clothes on. The number of institutions is steadily increasing where you will not find a single person running around naked or lying on the floor surrounded by urine and feces. On a higher functioning level, we now know that while reading and writing are useful skills, a person without them can still find his or her way about in the community along familiar routes, and can learn to handle public transportation. It was a cliche readily accepted by educators that only the mildly retarded were capable of any abstract thinking, of translating knowledge gained in one situation to another situation, and that of course implied that the others were incapable of making any decisions. This, too, has proven to be completely false. To be sure, in the traditional situation, whether at home, in school, or in the institution, every decision was made for persons with mental retardation; they had no opportunity of developing any capacity for making decisions. Today we know that even mentally retarded persons who may have difficulty in expressing themselves verbally with clarity nonetheless may well be able to make choices and act on the basis of these conscious choices, and that is what decision-making is all about.

However, it is not just our knowledge about the potential of the mentally retarded person that has changed. We have also gained some significant new insight regarding the requirements for functioning in a community setting. The traditional viewpoint focused on pointing out that, as life has become more complicated and more involved with mechanization and technology, retarded persons who were able to get along in the small community or rural area could no longer keep up with the increasing demands of modern living. There is increasing evidence that this is an oversimplification. Much of the new technology in effect assists the retarded person. He no longer needs to read the newspaper—he gets extensive information through radio and television, and does so with far greater effectiveness than a slow reader perusing a newspaper. Shopping in self-service stores is manageable for a person with very limited language, and experience has proven that even the subway system of New York City, which overawes the visiting stranger, can be handled by a youngster formerly rejected by school systems as incapable of profiting from education. It is, of course, not my intention to convey that the disadvantage of an intellectual deficiency can be discounted. Being retarded is a substantial handicap. But its consequences are by no means as sweeping as previously depicted, nor is the retarded person as inaccessible to remediation as had been assumed.

With this introductory and explanatory statement, I now can

address myself to the specific topic the Program Committee has assigned to me—"Preparation of the Retarded Individual for Adult Living." You will now readily see why I first of all have to stress that in pursuing this topic we must avoid starting with the traditional, preconceived notions as to what retarded persons cannot do, cannot achieve. Instead, we should start positively with regard to the kind of life a retarded person should be expected to lead, and the starting point for that would be the life pattern of the average person in your own country, be it in the city or in a rural area, in Jamaica, in Trinidad, or in Barbados, depending on the type of person for whom we are supposed to plan—and in this case this means his or her potential functional level, considering the degree of disability.

Let me give some specifics. As adults, retarded persons should master a higher level of self care, no longer just limited to toileting, washing, and dressing, but extending to such things as preparation of simple meals, awareness of time and time limits, understanding of health needs (proper clothing, basic diet, alertness to potential danger), and the ability to get about (whether it is in the immediate neighborhood, limited to traffic signals, or more extensive travel involving public transportation). They should develop an ability to communicate with others, and while we automatically think here of the fluent use of language, we have learned that individuals who have no speech at all can make themselves understood and can actually interact socially with others.

An important point in social relations with others is to learn the proper form of addressing and speaking with adults, and that of course implies that we take care of teaching this by example, by teaching retarded adults a different type of language use than what was appropriate for them when they were children. For ourselves, we take it for granted that the informality of endearing language we use within the family is not appropriate when dealing with others in public. Yet this cardinal rule of social conduct is almost always overlooked in dealing with retarded persons. As a result, they do not learn to use appropriate language with others in the community, and this faulty speech pattern immediately sets them apart—quite unnecessarily—as inadequate, peculiar, or, to be more precise, childish persons.

As I was preparing myself for my appearance today, I came across a statement in which a colleague of ours set down, clearly and succinctly, provisions for the development of acceptable behavior on the part of severely and profoundly mentally retarded residents in an institution. She said that towards that end, such individuals should

- live in as normal a way as possible, with their own living space and in a small group,

- be recognized as individuals; use of proper name, enjoyment of one's possessions, including one's own clothing, identify with one's family, etc.,

- live in a bisexual world,

- experience a normal daily rhythm (which does not imply a rigid time schedule), utilizing a variety of environments (for sleeping, eating, leisure, etc.),

- eat in a small group,

- receive special education and training in all areas of personal and social development,

- have the opportunity to try out all appropriate activities of daily living (household chores, handicrafts, and work activities),

- have leisure pursuits which are individualized and differentiated according to the time of year,

- have the opportunity to interact with a variety of people including their peers, and

- be able to choose between different ways of spending their free time.

While this specific list was written for retarded persons in institutions, it does not contain a single item that would not be of equal significance to mentally retarded young adults living with their own family or in a group home. Much of this, of course, one would hope school will begin to teach, but experience has taught us how much of this can also be managed at home, particularly since some of the newer training techniques in behavior modification have been adapted for use by parents in the family home.

In recent decades, behaviorists and educators working in the general field of human development have become very much interested in the concept of the peer group and its practical application. Perhaps one of the most exciting new developments in our field has been the introduction of this concept to strengthen programs of preparing mentally retarded young people for adult living. First in Sweden, then in other countries, a definite effort has been made to assist mentally retarded young people to organize themselves, not just for social activities, important as this is, but beyond such a program. The retarded young people learn to interact constructively with each other, learn to express themselves, learn how to carry on a discussion, to debate an issue, to formulate and state their own views, interests, and opinions, and to arrive as a group in an orderly process at certain recommendations. In some instances this has been done particularly successfully when the retarded young people had an opportunity to interact and meet with non-handicapped young people, and young persons with other types of handicap. The results have been totally astounding and, as a matter of fact, so surprising to even seasoned practitioners in our field that questions were raised whether indeed this was done by the retarded young people themselves, or suggested to them by their elders. This is not surprising, considering our past beliefs, our past images of the retarded person. It parallels a similar phenomenon: encountering a group of retarded young people neatly dressed, their hair well groomed, their behavior inconspicuous, people simply refuse to believe that these could be severely retarded persons, because of the past association of severe retardation with clothing appropriate for persons much younger in years, disheveled appearance, a running nose and drooling mouth, a silly grin, poor posture, ungainly obesity, and strange mannerisms—all characteristic of an inappropriate upbringing and a neglect that would not be tolerated for a non-handicapped person.

Let me give you one sample of statements young retarded persons have formulated for themselves in Sweden several years ago in the report of a conference that had brought them together under the auspices of FUB, the Swedish parent's association. Among the points they made were the following:

Leisure Time Activities

We found that:

We want to be together in small groups during our leisure time.

Dance evening ought not to be for more than 14-16 persons.

Under no circumstances do we want to walk in large groups in town.

To have better contact with leisure time leaders, we think they should be of the same age as we.

We have all agreed that we want more power of participation in decision-making, especially in planning and implementation of leisure time activities.

We all think one should decide oneself what to do during vacations.

Living Conditions

We found that:

We wish to have an apartment of our own and not be coddled by personnel; therefore we want courses in cooking, budgeting, etc.

We want the right to move together with the other sex when we feel ready for it, and we also want the right to marry when we ourselves find the time is right.

We who live in institutions and boarding homes have found that:

The homes should be small.

We want to choose our own furniture, and have our own furniture in the room.

We will absolutely not have specific hours to follow in terms of going out, returning, etc.

We want to have more personal freedom, and not as it is now in certain institutions and boarding homes where you have to ask for permission to shop for fruit, newspapers, tobacco, etc.

We who live at home have found that:

It is largely good, but one ought to move out when the time is right to a service sheltered apartment or hostel; one cannot for his whole life be dependent on his parents.

We want, however, to have our own key when we live at home.

Questions Concerning Work

We demand more interesting jobs.

We do not want to be used on our jobs by doing the worst and most boring tasks we do at present.

We demand that our capacity for work should not be underestimated.

We want that when we are working in the open job market, our fellow workers should be informed about our handicap.

We think that we should be present when our situation is discussed by doctors, teachers, welfare workers, foremen, etc. Now it feels as if they talk behind our backs.

We demand to have more information about our handicap, and the possibilities we have to enter the open market.

Last Day of Discussion

Today we have talked about what to do to improve the bad conditions we have found during the discussion Friday and Saturday:

We demand that continuous information should be given to the counties and communities, schools, sheltered workshops, and other institutions for our handicapped group about the prevailing bad conditions.

We demand also that much stronger information be given to people in general through newspapers, radio and TV.

We have elected today a committee of six members and two alternates with the following tasks:

The committee shall continuously receive reports about the decisions of the National Board of the Swedish Association for Retarded Children,

The committee shall work for the general public and pressure the authorities. (Nirje, 1969)

You will say that the group which produced this document surely was composed of mildly retarded young people, but that is not so. The group included persons who previously had been denied admission to special classes in the public schools. Furthermore, in a very significant demonstration in Israel, Dr. Chigier has successfully shown how to use the peer group approach to motivate and to prepare severely and profoundly retarded adults, previously considered as totally incapable of any structured, productive effort, for a work experience in the orchards. Specifically, Dr. Chigier first worked with this group of young people in a recreational program with only one purpose—to get group interaction and group cohesion among these individuals, who previously had largely led a solitary existence. Once he had reached that goal, he moved with the whole group into the orchard and what he had anticipated came true—by supporting each other, by a group motivation, these severely handicapped young people for the first time gained a sense of accomplishment, a sense of being an adult, participating member in a society where productive effort was valued most highly. I might add parenthetically that a film Dr. Chigier prepared of this demonstration is available from the US Rehabilitation Service in Washington (Chigier, 1968).

I have tried to sketch out for you in my presentation some new approaches in the preparation of retarded young people for adult living. But at best I have presented only a small segment, a very partial picture. A few weeks ago my husband participated in a small conference that was to project a picture of mental retardation in the year 2000. In this discussion he stressed several times the urgent need to improve our techniques of early intervention, of improving the assistance we should give today to the families of severely handicapped infants and very young children. Some members of the group commented impatiently that what was needed was to think "long range" to the year 2000. My husband answered that that was precisely why he was so worried about early intervention, because children born within the next few months would be in their 25th year by the year 2000, and our job was to give them the best possible preparation for a meaningful life as adult citizens in our communities.

Jean Vanier, whose vision, faith, and wisdom resulted in the creation of some 45 small homes in nine countries around the world for handicapped men and women who were either roaming the streets, locked up in asylums, or just living idly, in a recent speech made an observation that sums up better than I could what I have tried to convey to you. He said:

> A man or woman can only find peace of heart and grow in motivation and creativity if he or she finds a meaning to life. If handicapped people are there only to be helped and can bring nothing to others, then they are condemned to a life of simply receiving, of being the last, the most inferior. This will necessarily bring them to depression and a lack of confidence in themselves. This in turn will push them into anguish and make them aggressive towards themselves and others. For them to find real meaning in life, they must find people who sense their utility, their capacity for growth and their place in the community and in the world. (Vanier, 1974)

Jean Vanier has given us the challenge. Will we be ready to meet it?

Chapter 9

The Mentally
Retarded Child Today—
The Adult of Tomorrow*

Whether the retarded children of today can be the effective adults of tomorrow will depend on the extent to which they have the opportunity to benefit from integrated experiences. Traditionally the schools have been exclusive, refusing to accept children with special problems. It was the physicians, not the educators, who started what today is called special education. Professor Jack Tizard, whose untimely death prevented his hoped-for participation in this Symposium, said already twenty-five years ago that the next major progress in special education of handicapped children had to come from general education, from the regular schools. By this he meant that schools would have to be more receptive to accepting children with handicaps and learning problems. Significantly, one of the last assignments he had before his death was a study for OECD (Organization for Economic and Cultural Development) on the vocational preparation of handicapped children, in the course of which he and the other members of the study group became aware of what is undoubtedly the most sweeping program for educational integration of all handicapped children, in development since 1971 throughout Italy. The League's former president, Yvonne Posternak, has documented this development in a report available from OECD (Posternak, 1979).

For developing countries, here is an issue of extreme importance. If they follow the advice of many professors of education

---

* Symposium of ILSMH, San Juan, Puerto Rico, 1979

and ministry of education officials, they will repeat history and build a school system which segregates handicapped children from their peers in the ordinary schools, and once such a system is created, it is indeed difficult to make changes, as has most recently been demonstrated by the report of the Warnock Committee to the British Government.

The foregoing comments have sketched out some basic actions that need to be given consideration if we want to enable children with mental retardation to be better prepared for assuming their roles as adults of tomorrow.

It is to that second phrase in the title of our Symposium—The Adult of Tomorrow—that we must now turn our attention. What do we have in store for our handicapped children as they reach adulthood, and what steps do we have to take to help them move forward?

Most appropriately, the 1979 International Year of the Child will be followed by the International Year for Disabled Persons, proclaimed for the year 1981 by a Resolution adopted by the General Assembly of the United Nations on December 16, 1976. The Resolution set forth the following five objectives:

(1) Helping disabled persons in their physical and psychological adjustment to society;

(2) Promoting all national and international efforts to provide disabled persons with proper assistance, training, care and guidance, to make available to them opportunities for suitable work and to ensure their full integration in society;

(3) Encouraging study and research projects designed to facilitate the practical participation of disabled persons in daily life, for example by improving their access to public buildings and transportation systems;

(4) Educating and informing the public of the rights of disabled persons to participate in and contribute to various aspects of economic, social and political life; and

(5) Promoting effective measures for the prevention of disability and for the rehabilitation of disabled persons.

It is important for us to keep in mind that this Resolution was written with reference to the entire spectrum of disabled persons, the vast majority of whom become disabled after they have reached adulthood. Looking therefore at the Resolution's first point, helping disabled persons in their physical and psychological adjustment to society, it is apparent that persons with mental retardation face special problems which require a long range program of special assistance from us.

The first of these problems was pointed up by Ann Shearer at the 1978 World Congress of the International League in Vienna when she said that mentally retarded persons, seen as misfits, are too often caught in a half-world between childhood and adulthood, fitting into neither, frozen into a continuous state of becoming prepared to enter adult life, yet not enabled to reach it. This is a formidable societal barrier which we must seek to remove (Shearer, 1978).

The second obstacle refers to the fact that within the total disability group, persons with mental retardation have traditionally been a minority within a minority. All too frequently, persons with other handicaps have successfully objected to the inclusion of a mentally retarded person in "their" programs. Reversing the attitudes and value judgements that have led to this "pecking order," this rejection of mentally retarded persons as inferior within the disability group, requires strong and determined help from organizations such as the International League and all its member associations.

The third obstacle is perhaps the most pervasive, and, at the same time, the one least clearly recognized. The professional literature dealing with the efforts in recent years of integrating retarded persons into the community alleges time and again that there is a strong and pervasive resistance on the part of your neighbors and mine (the common people) to having such persons live among them. However, the actual experience in the United States and in other countries negates this assertion. Where mentally retarded individuals have an opportunity to live like the rest of us in the community, they have been met with acceptance, even in places where initially there was resistance to their moving into the neighborhood. Once people actually encounter retarded persons, they are frequently not just tolerant but sympathetic and supportive, as has been so well documented by Robert Perske in this Symposium.

The prejudicial attitude does not rest with the common man, the man on the street, but rather with a small but vocal group of opinion makers, textbook writers, research workers, and administrators who, for some reasons that have yet to be explored and explained, feel impelled to denigrate and downgrade the potential as well as the actual achievements of persons with mental retardation. It is they who continue to talk about individuals incapable of responding to either education or rehabilitation, who stress disability rather than potential, who make their low expectations into self-fulfilling prophecies, who recommend policies that are exclusive rather than inclusive, denying access to programs because they presume the applicant to be incapable of sufficient progress.

Lest you feel that I am overstating the case, let me relate to you that in England recently a highly regarded psychiatric textbook was published with such grossly denigrating description of persons with mental retardation that a British advocacy group, the Campaign for the Mentally Handicapped, felt impelled to mount a protest action resulting in hundreds of signatures, resulting in turn in the publishers' promise that corrections would be made. In the United States, a group of well-known research workers in the field of psychology issued a statement claiming that in severe and profound retardation, limits of educability are encountered which preclude any program of training and education as futile (Partlow Review Committee, 1978). The National Association for Retarded Citizens recognized the seriousness of this situation and issued a strong Resolution in support of a developmental approach which is firmly based on the knowledge, not just the belief, that there is no human being who does not possess the capacity to grow and develop. The Center of Human Policy at Syracuse University responded to the psychologists' challenge with a manifesto entitled *The Community Imperative* which refuted point by point the psychologists' assertions (Center of Human Policy, 1979).

I have dwelt on this matter at such length because I hope that the discussions of this Symposium will address themselves very specifically to this issue and assist our member associations around the world to understand this problem and to develop appropriate action programs in much the same way that racial prejudice and the misinformation underlying it must be met head-on.

In our rapidly developing field it is urgent to spread new knowledge, to update textbooks, and to take positive steps to use this new knowledge effectively in day to day programs and services.

The 1968 Jerusalem Congress, at which the International League launched the Declaration of the Rights of the Mentally Retarded Persons, was followed by the League's 1972 Congress in Montreal with the challenging theme, "Suit the Action to the Word." What I am trying to convey to you is that this challenge is still confronting us; it is laid out carefully and well in the League's publication *Step-by-Step*, guidelines to implementing the Declaration on the Rights of Mentally Retarded Persons (ILSMH, 19?8b).

It may appear at first that these comments pertain only to countries with well established services for retarded children and adults, but this is not so. Observations of the international scene during the past twenty years have brought to light numerous instances where the so-called developing countries received in good faith and acted on information which no longer reflected acceptable practices. This Symposium must give careful consideration as to how the International League could strengthen and safeguard avenues of information that will help our member associations to assume effective leadership in their countries. Obviously, the League's collaborative arrangements with the United Nations and its Specialized Agencies, as well as with the international voluntary organizations concerned with disability, can provide a basis for extending and strengthening the channels of communication.

Within the framework of this brief introductory paper it is obviously not possible to deal adequately with what has remained, almost everywhere, the most difficult problem in planning for the adult persons with retardation—namely, appropriate employment or meaningful occupation. I would like to single out a few highlights.

For many workers in the field the sheltered workshop is the appropriate place of occupation for all of those who cannot work independently or find places in open employment. Recently, in one of the Scandinavian countries, we encountered among many of our colleagues the presumption that even for the moderately (middle level) retarded persons sheltered workshops would not be available, and "day centers" would be organized for them.

In contrast, speaking at the ILO Regional Seminar on Vocational Rehabilitation of the Mentally Retarded held last year in Jamaica, George Soloyanis emphasized the need to move away from "the stereotyped thinking which suggest[s] that the best and most comprehensive programs for retarded persons consist primarily of special education or training, then placement into a sheltered workshop." Accordingly, he laid out twenty-four work opportunities suitable for retarded persons which are in fact being undertaken somewhere in the world.

Because there has been a great deal of confusion about it, I would like to make specific reference to agricultural work. It came into bad repute as an occupation for retarded persons, particularly in the USA, because in many instances the large farms, attached to institutions serving several thousands, utilized what could only be called slave labor, without any thought of vocational preparation and future placement. However, in recent years the National Society for Mentally Handicapped Children (NSMHC) has developed a comprehensive agricultural training center, Lufton Manor, in southwest England. In the context of our Symposium it is worth noting that the Director, David Carter, has served as ILO consultant in several African countries (Carter, 1976).

At the same Congress, in Ann Shearer's presentation on "Meeting Vocational and Social Needs," various schemes of on-the-job training were mentioned, including one I want to highlight because of its simplicity of approach. In the "Pathway scheme" first promoted by the NSMHC in South Wales a few years ago, a small sum of money is offered to an ordinary, experienced worker, called a "foster worker," to guide a handicapped employee through his or her first month of employment, and the employer is guaranteed a grant to cover the first three months of wages (Shearer, 1978).

I have selected this particular example of innovative work placement and training because it seems to deal so effectively with the total employment situation, i.e., also assisting the retarded worker in handling the social and environmental aspects of the job, the area where failure most frequently originates. Obviously this is a scheme that can be adapted easily to any type of work situation.

Looking back over the past three decades since our movement on behalf of retarded persons came into existence, one can identify many significant events, such as, for instance, the founding of the International League. Yet I venture to say that nothing has been as impressive and as promising as the emergence of the person with mental retardation as an *active participant*, not only in the planning for his or her own present and future, but increasingly also as a person concerned about the well-being of others.

Chapter 10

Having Faith
in the Potential
of Communities*

The 1970s brought recognition that retarded children grow up to become adults living in the community, thereby necessitating a radical re-thinking of services. We saw the parents' insistent demand for educational and vocational training of their children come to reality in Chapter 766 in Massachusetts, and in 1975 nationwide with PL 94-142, the Education of All Handicapped Children Act. New federal legislation stressed the importance of community living—and I purposely use that word rather than deinstitutionalization—and, finally, the 1970s brought us another important development of crucial significance to the topic of this conference, the development of *self-advocacy*, a concept which rapidly became an action program extending throughout all areas of disability. The importance of these self-advocacy developments for this conference is obvious, because for the first time we see a coming together, an interest in collaborative action on the part of disability groups which previously had been unwilling to talk to each other.

But what about the community and its response to all these developments? Here we need to establish a clear difference between your neighbor and mine, John Q. Public, the Man-in-the-Street, and certain community institutions, public services, or ordinances such as those related to zoning. As far as the average citizen is concerned, the acceptance of persons with mental retar-

---

* *Presented at the Conference on Opportunities in Community Life, Holyoke, Massachusetts, 1985*

dation (the field in which I have been specifically involved for the past 25 years) and those with other disabilities has been phenomenal. People with severe—and that means obvious and visible—disabilities are moving freely through the community, shop in the supermarkets, ride the buses and increasingly the airplanes, visit the beaches, and attend movies and ball games; and they are doing this as individuals, not in large, labeled groups.

In all of this, Chapter 766 and Public Law 94-142 have been of crucial significance because in thousands of homes throughout our state, in millions of homes throughout the nation, parents hear from their own children the news that people with disabilities are joining all aspects of community living. To come specifically to the point of this evening's discussion, I do not just have "Faith in the Potential of Communities," I have proof of it, and if you just look around and about, you will see it, too. Indeed, I know you have and that is why you are here.

Obviously, there are problems, but we encounter problems in all aspects of living. If you want to encounter real prejudice, bigotry, and lack of acceptance, watch when conflict arises in one of our churches, for instance. A great deal is made of zoning problems, yet within the past year in my own community the objections to a small, privately run nursery school in a residential section were just as strong as those pertaining to the establishment of a community residence for persons with mental retardation. Zoning fights can be disagreeable and attract undue attention, but what is vastly more important is that once the fight is over, once the community residence is established, be it a group home, apartment, or other accommodation, in the overwhelming majority of cases throughout the country there are no further hostile manifestations, but rather a slow, gradual acceptance by the community at large, and not infrequently a few very wonderful, strong expressions of support and friendship. Further, there is now overwhelming evidence from official, carefully compiled reports from various parts of the country that property values do not decrease when persons with a disability join a neighborhood, nor is there a "flight" or moving away on the part of the neighbors (Jaffe and Smith, 1986). I can tell you, by the way, that this has been the experience also in other countries, both in Europe and in South America.

There are, of course, problems; there is work to be done. Bureaucrats, who always like things big, still insist on community facilities which are too large in size. In various states it has been amply demonstrated that smaller sized groups can be effectively and economically cared for in apartments or one-family homes. The continuity, and that often means the quality, of programs in the community is endangered when the state bureaucracy insists on paying the care staff an inadequate wage, often less than it pays in its state residential institutions. Questions of accountability and of monitoring need to be better worked out. And above all, there needs to be better coordination between state and local agencies, but all those are technical details in which citizens can participate in resolving.

Having faith in the potential of communities is not enough. We must aggressively assert our role in making sure that the bureaucracy is functioning adequately, is fulfilling the policy and philosophy of the state. Anybody who will take the time to look at the report the Governor of Massachusetts promulgated in 1966 as a result of the Kennedy legislation for comprehensive state planning (PL 88-156) can see how far the Department of Mental Health has fallen behind.

However, in spite of all these drawbacks and deficiencies, and they are considerable and cry out for remedy, I continue to have an optimistic outlook for the future. My optimism is largely based on the latest but potentially the strongest component of the disability reform movement, and that is the growing, ever more effective participation of persons with a disability. I wish there was time for me to relate to you the excitement that pervaded the large, multistoried assembly hall of the Kenyatta Congress Center in Nairobi, Kenya, two and a half years ago when, in the presence of 700 people coming from some 70 countries around the world, a group of persons with mental retardation (some of whom had been confined in state institutions for 30 years or more), themselves representing eight different countries and languages, presented to a plenary session of an international congress on mental handicap their own ideas and recommendations for the future. Subsequently, through the help of the professional interpreters for the Congress, the group responded to spontaneous questions from this international audience. If that can be done in a multi-national, multi-language, multi-racial international meeting, why is it not done in your community? And if it isn't, what can you, your friends, your organization, do to help persons with severe disabilities to represent themselves adequately, and to participate in community affairs? What will we do to translate this into action? Faith and Works, I believe, are the words to remember.

PART V

Employment and Rehabilitation

Chapter 11

International Perceptions of the Employment and Rehabilitation of Persons with Developmental Disabilities*

Before I can move into the topic area assigned to me, I need to make some clarifying statements about terminology. I strongly support the concept of developmental disabilities, particularly in its present, broader definition. As you will recall, as established by the US Congress in 1970, it originally only encompassed mental retardation, cerebral palsy, and epilepsy (autism was added somewhat later), until in 1978 the broader definition was adopted, which depends not on diagnostic entities but rather on extent and degree of functional impairment or limitation.

Internationally, however, this is not yet a generally accepted term and certainly not one identical to the US definition. On the other hand, the term mental handicap is synonymous with what is called in the US mental retardation; hence, the International League of Societies for Persons with Mental Handicap (ILSMH) is the international counterpart of the Association for Retarded Citizens/USA and the Canadian Association for Community Living. Altogether, this array of terminology (mental deficiency, mental retardation, mental handicap, intellectual disability, intellectual handicap, learning difficulties, and now developmental disabilities) clearly signifies that we are in an era of change. We are moving farther away from the labeling of persons and instead

---

*General Assembly, ILSMH, Mexico City, 1988

speak of conditions, and we increasingly recognize that in many instances not even that is necessary. May I say that the Canadian Parent Association is quite ahead in this regard by dropping the diagnostic term mental retardation, and substituting for it a goal, a functional direction: community living.

Let me now turn to the question of employment and rehabilitation from an international perspective, our topic for this morning. It is significant that the first Symposium of the International League, meeting in Frankfurt, Germany, in February 1966, dealt with sheltered employment and mental retardation. The League had been organized in 1960 as a European body, becoming international in scope and in name in 1962 when the American, Canadian, and a few other parent associations joined the European group. Hence the Frankfurt Symposium on Employment was an early effort of the League, limited to highly industrialized countries. It was greatly influenced on the one hand by a 1964 International Seminar on Sheltered Employment of the International Society for Rehabilitation of the Disabled (now Rehabilitation International), and, on the other hand, by two international documents. One was the Universal Declaration of Human Rights, adopted and proclaimed by the General Assembly of the United Nations in 1948, but unfortunately hardly known in this country despite its far reaching significance. Article 22 in substance proclaims the following:

> Everyone, as a member of society, has the right to social security and is entitled to realization . . . of the economic, social and cultural rights indispensable for his dignity and the free development of his personality.

Article 23 provides the following:

> Everyone has the right to work, to free choice of employment, to just and favorable conditions of work and to protection against unemployment . . . the right to equal pay for equal work . . . the right to form and join trade unions for the protection of his interests. (UN, 1948)

The second international document was ILO's Recommendation

99, made by the 1955 General Conference of the International Labour Organization, a Recommendation Concerning Vocational Rehabilitation of the Disabled. Two points of this recommendation are to be noted. Paragraph 1b stated:

For the purpose of this Recommendation the term "disabled person" means an individual whose prospects of securing and retaining suitable employment are substantially reduced as a result of physical or mental impairment.

Point 2 stated:

Vocational rehabilitation services should be made available to all disabled persons, whatever the origin and nature of their disability and whatever their age, provided they can be prepared for, and have reasonable prospects of securing and retaining, suitable employment. (ILO, 1955)

The Frankfurt Symposium in its recommendation adopted the following concept of sheltered employment, formulated by the earlier (1964) International Seminar:

Sheltered employment is to be understood as productive, remunerative employment of any type, supplied under conditions specially designed to meet the temporary or permanent employment needs of handicapped people. (ILSMH, 1967a)

The League Symposium added that extending such sheltered employment to retarded persons was a matter of right, rather than charity. The following year, in 1967, the League held a Symposium in Stockholm on "Legislative Aspects of Mental Retardation." Its conclusions (ILSMH, 1967b) went beyond the right to sheltered employment and asserted the mentally retarded person's rights to economic security, to a decent standard of living, to perform productive work or to engage in any other meaningful occupation. A year later, the Stockholm Symposium's conclusions on "Individual Rights" were adopted by the League's World Congress in Jerusalem as a *Declaration on the General and Special Rights of the Mentally Retarded* (ILSMH, 1968), and in December 1971 this Declaration was adopted by the General Assembly of the United

Nations, with no dissenting votes, entitled the *Declaration on the Rights of Mentally Retarded Persons*. One of its provisions states the following:

> The mentally retarded person has a right to economic security and to a decent standard of living. He has a right to perform productive work or to engage in any other meaningful occupation to the fullest possible extent of his capabilities. (UN, 1971)

Against the background of these international declarations, what is the actual situation today?

A few years ago while on a consultation trip to Austria, we were taken to a large modern vocational school in Vienna by staff members of the Lebenshilfe, the Austrian parents association. After years of effort they had succeeded in getting approval of the education authorities, both local and state, for the establishment of an experimental project in work training of adolescent pupils with mental retardation. In Austria, as in various other European countries, there still is for each trade a hierarchical ladder from apprentice to journeyman to master, and the project we were to see had installed within this big vocational school, for graduates from special education classes, three apprentice shops in carpentry, house painting, and locksmithy. We were very much impressed with what we saw in terms of the intensity of instruction, the insistence on a high grade performance, and the eventual quality of the finished work. To be sure, the young people were selected from those with mild and moderate degrees of retardation, but even that was unheard of in Austria. However, to the school's surprise, these handicapped students, who could never have gained admission there in the ordinary way, by far exceeded everyone's expectations.

Recently we inquired from one of the Austrian colleagues who had taken us there how things had progressed in the intervening years. Here is his report.

> My general feeling is that there hasn't been any exciting development since the Lehrwerkstatte (apprenticeship training). After five years of this project the outcome is obvious—and was actually positively pre-

dicted at the outset. Yes, it is possible to train persons with a mental handicap in various trades. And yes, it is also possible to find satisfying work for most of them, and satisfied employers and colleagues as well. But in a way the project and the thinking of Lebenshilfe Wien hasn't developed beyond what it was set up to do. That is to say, there are no attempts at training people in regular training sites rather than this special training site.

And while the Berufsschule (Trade School) was enthusiastic and experimental in the beginning, they have now established this routine of a special class in the regular setup. While the rest of Austria is beginning to move towards integrated schooling, they have not moved on, although they were real pioneers in the beginning. The project has remained a project—no other comparable setups spreading through Vienna or Austria, no real impact so far, except for the people it concerned.

Certainly it has been around long enough for the competent people to know and find out about. The rest—to a very large degree—is still sheltered workshops, Beschaftigungstherapie (Occupational Therapy), and some (little) sheltered employment in regular workplaces. (Spudich, 1988)

In other words, the unquestionable success of the project has failed to convince the vocational establishment that it should be replicated many times over—prejudice and fear of change in a well established system of trade training won out.

Compared with Austria, England for many years was much more aggressive both in schooling and work training of youngsters with mental handicap, albeit in totally segregated facilities. Here is what a well-informed British colleague wrote when I queried him as to his impressions of recent developments in employment and rehabilitation for young people with mental handicap.

I am glad that you are looking for impressions, rather than statistics, as the latter are hard to find. There is much talk (progressive, or maybe just fashionable) about finding better alternatives to our traditional provision—the Adult Training Center (ATC), or Social Education Centre. However, the implementation of these ideas has yet had little impact on actual service provision.

A number of models have been demonstrated as improvements on the ATC—though with the one possible exception of supported employment they all have flaws. One model is the cooperative venture (known here as a "co-op") where most of the workers are joint owners. This type of business attracts funding both from government and charitable bodies more readily than straight commercial undertakings. The Gillygate bakery in York is a long-established example, which you may have read about in our book, "Building Community." A recent addition is Rowanwood, a small co-op in an industrial unit in Cambridge: what most appeals to me about this venture is that the product—beautiful sculpted wood panelling—is at the high-prestige end of the market, in contrast to the indifferent concrete slabs which are so often regarded as the appropriate product of schemes involving people with learning difficulties.

A similar kind of project is the work training scheme. Most quoted example here is Applejacks, a cafe in North London, staffed mainly by people with learning difficulties, though each person for only a limited training period. The voluntary group which set it up went to a lot of trouble to avoid tell-tale and stigmatizing signs, and locally it just has a reputation as a good place for a cheap lunch.

MENCAP's Pathways employment placement services, and similar schemes, appear to have very variable success from area to area . . . My impression is that these services tend to feed people into the jobs like street cleaning and hospital portering, which though they may have great social value, are amongst the least socially valued.

The introduction of supported employment, with the extension of Marc Gold and Associates to this country, is sending shock waves across the more aware of our service planners and managers, but this work is still at the very early stages, so again the effect is, as yet, more on thinking than on actual services.

Meanwhile, new Government legislation is set to impede progressive developments. In relation to employment opportunities, probably the most significant policy is the enforced privatisation of local government services, which will deny enlightened local authorities from building employment opportunities for people with disabilities into the services which they have provided directly. (Dowson, 1988)

Unfortunately, time limitations force me to cut short these accounts of recent developments in other countries. Let me just close with a brief quote from a report I received from Dr. Renee Portray, President of the Belgian parents association and mother of a young man with Down's Syndrome who for many years has put in a full day's work at the International League's Brussels headquarters. She reports:

We have a large number of sheltered workshops but they all tend to keep the best workers and the least handicapped and refuse those considered as not enough productive. There is no training allowed in the workshops!
The adults refused in the sheltered workshops go to "day centers." Some are quite good and try to give a meaningful occupation. Others need improvement. And there is a shortage of day centers. (Portray, 1988)

To sum it all up—we have the know-how, we have far reaching policies, far sighted declarations, but aside from some shining bright spots, employment and rehabilitation leave much to be desired. And that, it would seem to me, applies to our country as well.

PART VI
Human Rights

Chapter 12

Human Rights:
New Trends in Legislation and
Action Around the World*

On a sunny autumn day in 1921 an English woman was sitting on top of the mountain of Saleve, overlooking Geneva. Her name was Eglantyne Jebb, and for years she had devoted her life to helping the world's needy and handicapped children. Whether they were victims of the war or victims of poverty, crippled by disease or by the lack of proper care, these children and their plight were her concern and that of the voluntary organizations in many countries which, in no small measure due to her inspiration, eventually came to found the International Union for Child Welfare.

But on that afternoon Eglantyne Jebb's mind was not concerned with problems of organization; rather she was taking stock of what she and her friends and colleagues in the charitable movement in many countries had been accomplishing in appealing for public generosity to aid unfortunate children. And suddenly an inspiration came to her—suddenly she saw that what really mattered was that help should come to these children as a matter of right, not as a consequence of generosity for charity's sake. And so she sketched out—sitting on this mountain top—a statement of principles that was destined to become part of a Magna Carta for the world. Entitling her document a "Declaration of the Rights of the Child," she developed principles affirming to all children a full opportunity to develop, to grow up under their parents' protection, to be assured protection from illness and exploitation, and, if handicapped, to receive the needed special

* Jamaica Council for the Handicapped, Kingston, Jamaica, 1974

care and education.

In the headquarters of the International Union for Child Welfare in Geneva there hangs an impressive array of state documents, in many languages, bearing the signature of reigning kings and queens and of other great national leaders such as Mahatma Ghandi, all of whom had pledged themselves to support of this Declaration. But although in 1924 the Assembly of the League of Nations adopted this document, subsequently it became painfully evident that the world was not ready for this forward looking and yet so simple Declaration. The disruptions caused by the worldwide economic depression of the 1920s and by World War II and its preceding years of totalitarianism have unfortunately overshadowed the singular achievement of this woman whose Declaration of the Rights of the Child had found world-wide acceptance.

What was so significant about the Geneva Declaration was not the fact that it spoke of services for the handicapped—various countries long before had adopted specific programs such as those dealing with industrial accidents, work related illnesses and the like; what was significant was that it asserted the right to assistance for all handicapped children without qualifications, simply as a consequence of their existence as human beings (Charlott and Morier, 1968).

World War II brought with it bitter destructiveness towards human beings on a scale never before experienced, but it also gave rise to the development of rehabilitation techniques and of new insights that human bodies and human minds, even those most severely damaged, could be mended. And with it came a new appreciation of the individual human being, of the integrity of what we call a person. These new insights led, in the early days of the United Nations' existence, to the promulgation of the Universal Declaration of Human Rights as a common standard of achievement for all people and all nations.

Interestingly, it took another eleven years before the United Nations General Assembly, in 1959, returned to the Geneva Declaration as approved by the League of Nations. In its more modern rephrasing, Principle 5 states that "the child who is physically, mentally or socially handicapped shall be given the special treatment, education, and care required by his particular condition." This principle reinforced what had already been stated in Article 26 of the Universal Declaration of Human Rights, namely, that the right to education applies to all persons. But when in the following year representatives of ministries of education around the world joined together in Geneva for the 23rd International Conference on Public Education with the education of mentally retarded children as their primary focus, they found that, in actual practice, public school systems still tended to exclude large numbers of handicapped children, particularly those with mental handicaps.

Many years have passed since that 1960 Conference, whose published proceedings, with reports from 71 countries, serve as a good baseline to assess trends and progress in the intervening years. And progress there has been, progress of such dimensions that within the time allotted me I can only briefly enumerate the main developments incorporated either in statutory or regulatory changes.

1. Special education, at least that for the more severely handicapped, in the past was frequently administered by other than the regular education authorities. This was justified by the contention that the more severely handicapped could only be "trained" but not educated, and such training was best assigned to health or welfare authorities. England was such a country where the classes for the "educationally sub-normal" were under the school authorities, whereas the training centres for the "severely subnormal" were under the health authorities. Five years ago legislation was introduced which transferred responsibility, as of 1971, for education of all children (including those in residential care) to the education authorities. Similar developments have taken place elsewhere, such as in the Scandinavian countries.

2. In many countries, statutes decreed a shorter period of education for handicapped children. They were admitted to school at a later age than non-handicapped children and their right to schooling ended earlier. In this regard we have an almost

complete reversal, because the legislative trend is now to make special provisions for very early pre-school services for handicapped children, and to prolong the time in which they are entitled to public education.

3. Even where special education was offered for handicapped children, attendance was often left to the discretion of the parents. However, more recently there has been a trend to make schooling compulsory also for handicapped children.

4. In the past it was common to have separate educational legislation for the various disability groups, often with quite different provisions one from the other. The practical difficulties of dealing with multiply handicapped children have resulted in a trend to think of the total group in global terms. This has been reinforced by a growing insight that the child is more important than the handicap, and that the old practice of labeling children by disability was damaging rather than helpful.

5. Not necessarily by legislative action but by regulation, there is a trend to bring special education closer to or actually into general education, to have special education teachers meet general teacher standards and enjoy general teacher benefits.

6. Mainstreaming, to use an American expression, is increasingly emphasized, meaning that many more handicapped children than previously was thought possible are attending public school classes with help of special instructors, or in any case are taught in public school buildings and participate to the extent feasible in general school activities.

7. This necessitates, of course, that regular class teachers become better informed about the needs and capacities of handicapped children.

8. While all these preceding changes have originated with administrative or legislative provisions, a new and as yet quite unique

development can be reported from the United States. Parents of retarded children excluded from or never admitted to school have initiated legal action in the courts against the education authorities (alleging, for instance, violation of their children's constitutional rights to education) and have gained court rulings in favor of their children's right to education.

Major developments have also taken place in the field of work training and work placement. In 1955 the General Conference of the International Labor Organization (ILO) adopted Recommendation 99 concerning vocational rehabilitation of the disabled. Although ILO's original concern had been with the injured worker, the Conference broadened its scope considerably and stated that "vocational rehabilitation services should be made available to all disabled persons, whatever the origin and nature of their disability and whatever their age, providing they can be prepared for, and have reasonable prospects of securing and retaining suitable employment."

Progress in this field has been slower than in the field of education, and that is understandable because the right to schooling is much more readily accepted and implemented than the right to work. The following legislative developments can be highlighted:

1. Various attempts have been made to create greater work opportunities by forcing or inducing larger establishments to hire a proportion of handicapped persons.

2. A parallel effort has been to authorize the government to set aside a certain amount of its requirements for products to deal with the problem of job procurement for those in sheltered workshops or home industries.

3. By statute or by regulation, provisions have been made to relieve the employer, at least in part, of the special risks he encounters by hiring disabled people.

4. Legislation has been introduced protecting handicapped persons from discriminatory employment practices.

5. Sheltered workshops in the past were considered charitable enterprises and hence exempted from the supervision and regulations government maintains over industrial or trade establishments. The result was often gross exploitation of persons in such workshops, working a full day but receiving a mere pittance in wages. There is now an increasing tendency for the Ministry of Labor or other appropriate government agency, by law, regulation, or practice to establish procedures protecting the handicapped worker from exploitation, insisting on commonly accepted work safety rules, and enforcing minimum wage standards.

6. In the past, rehabilitation facilities were specialized by disability category and often were subject to different regulations and practices. The separation was especially sharp between facilities for the physically and the mentally handicapped. As in special education, the trend is towards a de-emphasis of disability categories in favor of larger, more industrialized mixed workshops, but with a growing preference for preparing the handicapped worker for employment on the open market.

The general trends just described with regard to education and rehabilitation programs are intimately related to mobility, and mobility in turn depends on a barrier-free environment. One major concern expressed in legislation has been the assurance of unimpeded access to public buildings. Relevant legislation has been introduced in many countries, backed by technological advances and a major program of public education. As my husband and I travel to various countries of the world, we are pleased to see more and more often the symbol of barrier-free architecture, the stylized wheelchair. Barrier-free access to buildings and within buildings deals with only part of the problem. Barrier-free transportation is a more difficult problem, increasingly recognized and yet rarely satisfactorily resolved.

Housing for the handicapped adult requires separate consideration. On the one hand it should provide barrier-free access to and within the housing unit, for instance, an apartment. But on the other hand, handicapped persons should be protected from unreasonable public health and safety restrictions. This is a particular problem in my own country, where there is a great concern with fire and safety protective devices which tend to dehumanize residential space—for example, in community group homes. The normalization principle as it has been developed by Bank-Mikkelsen in Denmark and Bengt Nirje in Sweden can provide here valuable guidelines.

There was a time when for the common man invalidity was closely associated with destitution, begging, and almsgiving, or even with confinement in a workhouse or poor-farm. The growing acceptance of income maintenance through social insurance and other social security measures is leading in an increasing number of countries to legislation which makes such financial support a matter of entitlement rather than a grant of charity.

What I have discussed so far pertains to the major program aspects in planning for handicapped persons. But there are other, more personal, more intimate aspects of living, where the handicapped person in the past has faced severe restrictions and humiliating discrimination, and none more so than the mentally handicapped individual. It is therefore significant and a matter of poetic justice, if not fulfillment of the biblical prophecy, that the last shall be first, that on December 20, 1971, the United Nations General Assembly, following an initiative of the government of France in the United Nations Social Development Commission, adopted without a dissenting vote the *Declaration on the Rights of Mentally Retarded Persons*.

The Declaration originated from a Symposium on Legislative Aspects of Mental Retardation, convened in Stockholm in 1967 by the International League of Societies for the Mentally Handicapped. The conclusions of that symposium, which by the way are available from the Secretariat of the League in Brussels, contain a section entitled "individual rights," with the following introduction:

The symposium considered that no examination of the legislative aspects of the problem of mental retardation would be complete without general consideration being given to the basic rights of the mentally retarded, not only from the standpoint of their collective rights and those of their families, but also from that of the individual rights of the retarded person as a human being. (ILSMH, 1967b)

There were some who regretted that the United Nations, in adopting this unusual Declaration of Rights, did not extend it to all handicapped persons, and indeed wherever the phrase mentally retarded person appears in the Declaration, it could as well be replaced by the term handicapped person. On the other hand, there are those who feel that if only the Universal Declaration of Human Rights were accepted as guidelines for governmental action, there would be no need for a separate Declaration.

That argument could well be extended to raising the question whether it really is necessary to have special legislation to assure education to handicapped children. Should they not derive this from the general school law? Certainly there is always danger in special legislation for a particular minority group. It may assure them some protection but it also sets them apart, and, furthermore, what yesterday was well-meant and well-applied protection can become tomorrow a discriminatory barrier.

We must be ever mindful that in some countries those who by most competent educational authority had been judged ineducable, based on seemingly flawless research studies, today are taught in special classes in the public schools, that individuals once described as vegetables (a term I deeply resent when used against a fellow human being), who were considered permanently non-ambulatory, are up and about, severely disabled, to be sure, but functioning in ways nobody thought possible. And in similar fashion, individuals once considered unemployable are today employed.

This sequence of events moved one of my colleagues to impress on his staff "in mental retardation you never say never," and that could be extended to our experience with handicapping conditions in general. This then must lead us to a cardinal rule about legislation in this field. To the extent that it deals with human beings, legislation must have flexible provisions, provide for growth, for change.

In the first quarter of this century, the eugenic scare panicked authorities into wholesale detention of the feeble minded. Today we calmly discuss that mentally retarded young men and young women are entitled to sexual fulfillment. The difference is that in the first quarter of the century our concern was with what had to be done *for* the deaf, *for* the crippled, *for* the mentally retarded. Over the past several decades we have seen handicapped persons increasingly take a hand in managing their problems, in expressing their views, in fashioning their life.

Over the past several years, we have been able to witness this also in the field of mental retardation, where, first in Sweden, then in England, Canada, the United States, and undoubtedly some other places, mentally retarded young people have come together, have learned to express themselves, to interact socially among themselves and with other non-handicapped young people, and, finally, have successfully claimed the right to participate in decision making. Indeed, last Sunday a group of German rehabilitation workers visiting in Boston met up with the Mohawks, a social club of young and middle-aged retarded people who, and this may shock you, have hired themselves out as a consultant team on various occasions to advise organizations planning to start a workshop, a community residence, a recreation center. And why not? Nobody could deny that they are "experienced."

Many of you will say: "but surely this could only mean that these individuals were really not very much retarded." That is a strange, frustrating phenomenon in the field of handicap: whenever handicapped persons really succeed, really lift themselves way up, so many people are inclined to believe that they were not really greatly handicapped to begin with. What is the reason for this need to judge people as incompetent, incapable, to resist acknowledging progress?

I see here a very serious problem, because new insights, new educational methods and behavioral approaches, reinforced by the products of new technological advances, have begun and will continue to result in significant and often surprising progress in

individuals with most severe handicaps, either physical or mental.
Will we be ready to assist and further them? Or will our doubts
based on past misconceptions block their way?

Nobody has seen more clearly the connecting link between our
laws, our programs, our attitudes, and the human factor in the field
of handicap than Jean Vanier, whose creative mind is matched by
his human compassion. May I close with a few paragraphs from
a talk he gave at the International Conference on Social Welfare in
Nairobi, Kenya, last July, entitled "The Contribution of the Physically and Mentally Handicapped to Development":

> The handicapped people have all the rights of other men; the right to
> life, to medical and social help and to work. They are able, when this is
> recognized to develop in so many ways. With the right educational and
> work techniques, many can find their place in the world of work and
> become totally integrated in that world. I have seen men who at the ages
> of six were judged incapable of any growth working in a factory at the
> age of 20 and living quite autonomously. Others who were condemned
> to asylums, to beggary or to total inactivity are now finding fulfillment
> in artisanal work and enjoying life in the community. With care, loving
> attention and the right kind of technical help, many can find their place
> in society. But this is not the question I wish to treat: others have done
> it better than I could and besides, it is not central to my theme.
>
> Handicapped people, and particularly those who are less "able"
> are frequently endowed with qualities of heart which serve to remind
> so-called normal people that their own hearts are closed. Their simplic-
> ity frequently serves to reveal our own duplicity, untruthfulness and
> hypocrisy. Their acceptance of their own situation and their humility
> frequently reveal our pride and our refusal to accept others as they are.
>
> If we listen to them, then we, the so-called normal and valid people,
> will be healed of our unconscious egoisms, our hardness of heart, our
> search for power and for dissipating leisure. We will discover that love,
> communion, presence, community and deep interior liberty and peace
> are realities to be found and lived. We will discover that these can
> become the inspiration for all men. We will realize more fully that men
> are not machines or objects to be used, exploited, tyrannized, and
> manipulated by law and by organizations, but that each one is beautiful
> and precious, that each one in his uniqueness is like a flower which
> should find its place in the garden of humanity for the fulfillment and
> beauty of all mankind.
>
> If each one of us who hold responsible places in society pay

attention to the heartbeats of the smallest, the weakest and the companionless, then gradually we will make of our countries not lands of competition, which favor the strong and powerful, but lands of justice, peace and fraternity where all men unite and cooperate for the good of every man. (Vanier, 1974)

Chapter 13

Human Rights:
Myth or Reality*

Your program committee has asked me to discuss this morning the topic "Human Rights—Myth or Reality." Let me state right off my premise as pointedly as I can. There is no question that human rights for mentally retarded persons, young and old, *are a reality*, that they exist. That evidence is all around us. But there is also the reality that there are all too many people who keep on denying this reality, who call these human rights a myth, a fantasy, wishful thinking, and worse.

It is only fair to state that a number of people in this room, people who do care for and about retarded individuals, nevertheless hold this view and cannot accept the reality of human rights as it relates to the retarded person for whom they care.

Let me now hasten to add that to assert the *reality* of human rights is by no way saying that the implementation, the fulfillment of these rights, is an accomplished fact. These are indeed two different things, recognizing the reality of human rights for mentally retarded persons and then setting about implementing these rights on a day-to-day basis. The point that must be made forcefully is of course that we cannot possibly hope for any kind of implementation efforts from people who in the first place deny that such rights do exist, that mentally retarded individuals are endowed with the same human rights as the rest of us.

Next it must be stressed that there is a marked difference between *human* rights and *legal* rights. Legal rights are either derived from specific statutes or from basic pronouncements of the

---

* British Columbia Association for the Mentally Retarded, Victoria, British Columbia, 1976

judiciary, the courts. Human rights cover much broader ground. They grow out of the human existence itself, may be formulated by philosophers or pronounced by some body such as the United Nations. I refer you to the program of this conference, where on page 2 you will find reprinted the *UN Declaration on the Rights of Mentally Retarded Persons*, which, in the second paragraph specifically, speaks of reaffirming faith in human rights.

Most legal rights relating to persons involve human rights, but you only need to recall the terror regimes of Hitler in Germany to remember legal rights which were devoid of any humanity.

On the other hand, it is important to be mindful that in general even those human rights which lack the affirmation as legal rights can and do have a powerful influence on our lives, and in many instances determine our actions *as if* we were facing the mandate of a law.

What is the meaning of all of this, within the framework of the theme of this Conference? Let me start with a simple and yet most fundamental point: out of the human experience has come the recognition that human life can be equated with growth and development. There is no standing still; there may be processes of deterioration leading to death, but growth and development is *the* basic fact of human life, and the most basic human right derived from this is the *right* to grow and develop, the right to move from childhood to adolescence, from adolescence to adulthood. Human growth is not just a physiological process. It expresses itself in many different areas of human life. Traditionally, one of the most basic impediments in the life of retarded persons has been a persistent effort to deny this growth process. Some years ago your own Canadian Film Board called persons with mental retardation "Eternal Children." Nobel Prize winner Pearl Buck referred to her retarded adult daughter as "The Child Who Never Grew." And last evening John DuRand expressed his exasperation in seeing grownup men and women come to his workshop with Mickey Mouse lunch boxes. His example was well chosen, because the daily use of such an inappropriate lunch box does amount to a daily denial that the person carrying the box has a right to be seen as being a young man, or a young woman, and, quite obviously, this denial will manifest itself in many other ways. Again, let me refer to Mr. DuRand's slides we saw last night. In one instance he showed, very compellingly, how just the surroundings, the work environment, in which we place a retarded young adult can be damaging when it looks like a playroom rather than a work station.

At first blush this point may impress you as being far removed from anything as high sounding as a basic human right, yet ever more increasingly we have come to recognize the significance of a term educators have long been using: "age-appropriate." My husband likes to tell a story how, very early in his career as the Executive Director of the National ARC, he was taught the importance of this factor by the parent of a retarded child. He had spent the day visiting various facilities of the parent association in the State of South Dakota, and had been taken by the State President to his house for dinner. After an initial greeting, the lady of the house had gone to the kitchen to prepare dinner, and the children were playing outside, with the exception of the youngest, a boy with Down's Syndrome who had remained in the living room. The father excused himself to make some telephone calls, and in connection with this story it is important to mention that he had been totally blinded as an adult. In any case, as the father talked on the phone my husband spoke to John, the boy with Down's Syndrome, and to my husband's great satisfaction, after a while John climbed on his lap and they continued to chat. As the father hung up the phone he listened for a second and, with the acuity of hearing many blind persons develop to compensate for their loss of sight, he surprised my husband by saying "Doc—is that boy sitting on your lap?" And, without waiting for an answer, he added quite sharply, "John, you know where you should be. Go out and play in the yard."

My husband, who had been rather pleased that this child had responded so nicely to him, next got a lesson which he has never forgotten and which has helped him to understand a key problem in raising retarded children when the father said to him, "You must excuse my having spoken so sharply. I did not mean to embarrass you, but my wife and I became aware how we had not just accepted but encouraged in our retarded son a show of affection, hugging, and kissing, quite different from what was the case with our other boys. At the same time, our other children commented how John's babyish ways kept him from being accepted by the other kids in the neighborhood. So we, as a family, decided that just because John was very slow with his school work and physically awkward for his age there was no reason to treat him like a baby, and we all resolved to help him behave more like a nine-year old. And nine-year olds don't sit on stranger's laps! We feel it is of great importance that along with the love and affection of his family, we help him to get a social acceptance from the other children in the neighborhood—and it is working."

A long story about a rather simple matter, and yet my husband feels that there are only two or three other incidents in the many years of his work in the field of mental retardation which have been as helpful to him. I should add that this happened in 1958, and at that time you could have searched all the textbooks on mental retardation in Canada, the United States, and Britain, and in vain would you have looked for this basic insight into the growth needs of a child with Down's Syndrome.

There is a companion story—it was not much more than a week later when my husband visited a fairly large workshop in Cleveland, Ohio. This was one of the few workshops that had a separate section for men and women deemed to be too severely retarded for the regular workshop training, but who were occupied with some simple manual work, sitting around a table quite far removed from the rest of the workshop activities. My husband stood quietly at a distance, observing this group of severely retarded people, when he noticed a man in his late 20s get up from his place, walk around the table and put his arm around a young woman, patting her. The man returned to his place and my husband was quite disconcerted about what looked to him like aggressive sexual behavior and the consequences it could have. Just then another young woman at this table burst into tears because something had gone wrong with whatever she was occupied with and, lo and behold—the woman supervising this group got up from her place, walked around to the girl who was crying, put her arms around her, doing exactly what the retarded man had done a few minutes earlier. The connection between these two stories hardly needs to be elaborated. They both refer to this basic human right I mentioned before, the right to grow and develop, or, you might say conversely, the right not to be hindered in growth and development. And this serves me well as an introduction to discussion of an area that continues to evoke a great deal of controversy, not only among parents of retarded children, but also among workers in the field.

A very important part of our human existence is our sexual identification as a man or a woman, and the deep and abiding satisfaction we derive from relating ourselves to others as a man or a woman. Healthy sexual identification starts early in life; one learns to be a boy or a girl, in preparation of learning later on to be a man or a woman. Parents and others with responsibility for caring for retarded children became convinced that this was too difficult a problem for retarded people to handle and that the kindest and safest way was to keep them apart from sexual experience and heterosexual relationships.

Actually, experience has shown that what was sincerely meant as protection does not necessarily work out this way—inevitably, situations develop where it is essential for the young retarded person to know how to behave with members of the opposite sex in a socially acceptable way. And we now know that sex education can be given in a way that is appropriate even to the limited understanding of severely retarded persons.

This brings me to another extremely controversial question regarding the basic human rights of retarded people—namely, use of measures to control their sexual functioning. In recent years there has been—from all we can determine—an increase in hysterectomies performed on young retarded girls, some of them preadolescent, for the purpose of not only rendering them sterile but of relieving them and the family of concern with menstrual hygiene. In other cases, sterilization alone is performed.

In past decades, sterilization was deemed justifiable in the face of alarming information about the danger of genetic pollution. Today we not only recognize that most of this was misinformation; sterilization and, even more, hysterectomy is seen now as such a radical intrusion on a retarded person's right to bodily integrity that neither parent nor physician can give valid permission (excepting, of course, in medical emergencies which would require a hysterectomy for other reasons).

Does this mean that nothing can and must interfere with a retarded person's basic human right to relationship with the other sex, to marry and to have children? By no means. The Declaration on the Rights of the Mentally Retarded Persons has a very important clause in Article 7, which reads as follows:

> Some mentally retarded persons may be unable, due to the severity of their handicap, to exercise for themselves all of their rights in a meaningful way. For others, modification of some or all of these rights is appropriate. The procedure used for modification or denial of rights must contain proper legal safeguards against every form of abuse, must be based on an evaluation of the social capability of the mentally retarded person by qualified experts and must be subject to periodic reviews and to the right of appeal to higher authorities.

In other words, one can appeal to the court for sterilization, but the term "proper legal safeguards" would imply that the judge in each case would inquire whether less radical steps could be used, such as proper sex education and birth control measures.

It is not hard for me to guess that quite a few persons in this audience will respond with distinct impatience to all these elaborate measures of safeguarding the interests of persons who appear obviously incompetent in the exercise of common life patterns. Two important points need to be made here: the first one is that we have increasing evidence that in the past we have grossly underestimated the functional capacities of severely retarded individuals, and persons like John DuRand and Marc Gold are providing some of this exciting new evidence. The second point is that the presumed incompetence of severely retarded persons has been the direct result of our failure to teach them, and of our depriving them of stimulating environments, and nowhere is this more clearly demonstrated than in our traditional large institutions.

Our concern with basic human rights of mentally retarded persons has gained additional significance with recent developments, led, unfortunately, by some scholars in the fields of ethics in the USA but reflected in other countries as well. What we are witnessing are attempts to prove that human rights can safely be disregarded with profoundly retarded individuals because, so it is claimed, they are not to be considered *human*; and therefore there should be no prohibition against any measure of controlling them, including killing them. One of these scholars, Professor Joseph Fletcher, goes one step farther and claims that a second group, not quite so profoundly retarded, should be considered as "semi-humans," entitled only to minimal care and protection (Fletcher, 1972). Nor is this to be considered a purely philosophical argument among scholars. We have evidence freely given by physicians in leading hospitals that they have put infants to death for the only reason that they were afflicted with Down's Syndrome.

The key point I would like to put before you is this: once we deny basic human rights to any group of retarded people, we cannot avoid having opened a Pandora's box. We cannot avoid a general devaluation of all mentally retarded persons; indeed, this is but a first step down the path of Adolf Hitler's policies. Once we allow parents to sterilize their young retarded children on the basis of one set of circumstances we open the way to other measures directed at other types of cases, and the hysterectomy as a means of avoiding hygienic inconvenience is a telling example.

I have made references several times in the foregoing remarks to parents and their relationship to their retarded child. Lest I be misunderstood, I would like to add here some further comments on the great significance which I ascribe to the parent-child relationship, because one of the most deeply ingrained human rights in your country and mine is the right to live with one's own parents, in the protective circle of the family. Moreover, the past several years have brought us a great deal of compelling evidence that parents can and must assume a significant partnership role in any program sponsored by any agency on behalf of their children, particularly, of course, during their early years. I make a special point about this because often when I discuss with parent groups the rights of retarded persons, some parents inevitably raise the question "Do we as parents have no rights at all?" Most definitely, such rights exist and must be acknowledged; some of you heard me discuss, for instance, the new special education law in my State of Massachusetts, which spells out in great detail the right of parents not just to be informed but to *participate* in decision-making concerning the school program of their child. But this importance of the relationship between child and parents, and the great supportive value of the family situation must—in terms of the child—be seen as a basic human right to live with one's family, and this should imply a right for assistance to the family from the appropriate outside agencies so that the child can receive proper care. In other words, care away from home should take place only when all means have been exhausted to bring to the family necessary help. And as you are well aware, British Columbia, along with all other provinces, has barely scratched the surface in applying well known, proven measures of supporting a family in raising their retarded child at home. Rather, the Province, for its own convenience, prefers to maintain easily managed large institutions—with results I need not go into here.

There are, of course, situations when a child requires services outside the home, but they will always be clearly definable. But what about the family who for good and valid reasons is unable to take care of a child in the family unit? In such cases the basic human right of the child to live within a family situation should mean a right to be placed in a substitute home which provides, as much as possible, the security and acceptance which fosters individual growth. I realize that this is a point bitterly contested. But it is frankly untenable to speak of the overwhelming importance of the family home (and I agree with that) on the one hand, and, on the other hand, to move in the opposite direction and depend on the impersonal care of an institution when the family feels unable to cope with the child for an indefinite period. A time-limited stay for a specific treatment plan in an appropriate therapeutic institutional setting is, of course, another matter.

I have at various times this morning made references to problems of children and adults with Down's Syndrome, and I realize how unsatisfactory it is to talk about such intensively human issues in an abstract way. My husband and I have had the great fortune to be able to watch the growth and development of a large number of retarded children in various countries from early childhood into adolescence and adulthood, and this has given us a strong sense of optimism for what lies ahead. Therefore, I thought it would be appropriate if I share with you this morning the success story of a child with Down's Syndrome—in other words, of a child who in the opinion of some would not be considered a human being—and should either have been sent to an institution or done away with altogether.

I have chosen his story because toward the end I am referring to some of the problems we have discussed here this morning.

Jacques Dumont is a young man with Down's Syndrome in his early 20s. He lives in a large city in Belgium with his parents and younger brothers; in the office where he is employed he runs the addressograph and mimeograph machines, goes to the post office and the bank, prepares the morning and afternoon coffee, and is a helpful and trustworthy worker. He lives 15 minutes from the office and likes to walk home from work but also can use public transportation. He does his own personal shopping and independently calls up favorite relatives to invite himself to a meal. Growing up in a family with musical interests he enjoys opera and ballet, and not only listens himself to classical music but informs his mother of good radio programs. While his reading skill is minimal, listening to radio and television keeps him aware of current events, and at election time he knew for which candidate he wanted to vote and did so.

After his parents became involved in organizing a group home for mentally retarded young men and women, Jacques began to visit there independently, not just to socialize but to be helpful, for instance, with newcomers, whom he tries to make feel at home. He rides a bicycle, swims well, and has learned to ski. He has taken trips by train and plane by himself, and although he is rather shy, he has learned to handle social situations reasonably well. While he looks younger than his real age and his posture is not the best, his physique has without doubt been greatly aided by the opportunity to help on a farm during summers. Pitching hay and driving a tractor are not activities one usually considers appropriate for young people with his handicap but they have been right for him, and undoubtedly have substantially contributed to his physical development and self confidence.

The point is often made that while a young person like Jacques can manage in the protective environment of his parental home, he might easily feel "lost" in some other living situation in the community, such as a hostel or supervised apartment. Yet many of Jacques' present leisure activities are carried on independently. He attends on his own a swimming club; he purchases his own tapes and, having learned from his brother, records favorite radio programs; another hobby he enjoys doing alone is making woolen carpets. He needs no help in preparing a sandwich or other light snacks for himself.

In the past Jacques has fallen in love several times with non-handicapped young women, passing infatuations which left him sad. He knows he is an adult (and uses that word); someday he may want to establish his own household as other adults do. Now that he likes to visit in the nearby hostel, he might perhaps find a young woman there he may want to marry. Jacques will need help at that point in realistically grasping the demands of such a relationship, along with the problem of maintaining a household. Still, if having a separate household turns out to be too much of a challenge, the young couple may be satisfied to have their own quarters as part of a hostel or group home, at least at the beginning. In general it is assumed that men with Down's Syndrome are not capable of reproduction. Should tests prove the contrary, the question of pregnancy prevention would have to be discussed with the young couple in terms which they can understand.

It can be said that Jacques is more ready to live in such a situation than society is ready to provide protected work, suitable living arrangements, and, above all, supportive counseling. Undeniably, Jacques is a human being with considerable limitations, intellectual and physical, but they are not so severe nor are they as serious an obstacle to living in the community as is commonly assumed of persons with Down's Syndrome. But to me he is also a symbol of the value and effectiveness of organizations such as yours, and it is indeed appropriate that the office where he works so effectively is that of the International League of Societies for the

Mentally Handicapped, an organization with which you are affiliated by virtue of your membership in the Canadian Association for the Mentally Retarded.

I hope many of you are aware that the Declaration of Rights for Mentally Retarded Persons, adopted by the United Nations General Assembly in 1971 and reprinted in your program, was initially adopted three years earlier, in 1968, by the Jerusalem Congress of the International League of Societies for the Mentally Handicapped, based on the findings of an International Symposium on Legal and Legislative Problems in Mental Retardation held in Stockholm in 1967 (ILSMH, 1967).

The strength of the League lies in the fact that it brings together from some 60 countries parent organizations concerned with mental retardation, and it is on their combined wisdom, energy, resourcefulness and commitment that I pin my hopes for a brighter future which indeed will assure to all retarded citizens their basic human rights—not as a myth but as a reality.

PART VII

The Image
and
The Reality

Chapter 14

Public Acceptance
of the Mentally Retarded*

One way of measuring progress in the field of mental retardation is to consider the change in the direction of public efforts. In the early decades of this century, considerable publicity was given to the mentally retarded, but it was publicity that was overwhelmingly negative. Those were the days when ill-conceived and poorly conducted studies had raised the specter of a growing population of defective individuals who were supposedly reproducing themselves at a rapid rate, filling prisons, almshouses, hospitals, and mental asylums with their ever-increasing progeny. The impact of this publicity was fear, and this fear of the mentally retarded led to strong popular support of the measures proposed by those who considered themselves experts in this subject. Thus, much legislation was passed authorizing sterilization and even castration of defective individuals, and imposing sharp restrictions of civil rights. Custodial care, that is, life-long banishment from the community, was considered the best answer to the problem, and led in many countries to the construction and maintenance of institutions, usually hidden from the eyes of the public and providing a minimum standard of care.

Of course, there were notable exceptions to this; great pioneers demonstrated, at times in progressive institutional care, at times through special educational programs in some of the larger cities, what remarkable success could be achieved in programs directed at the educational rehabilitation of the mentally retarded of all grades. However, the total international picture at the time of the

---

* ILSMH World Congress. Paris, 1966

second World War was overwhelmingly still one of public rejection of the mentally retarded, a rejection nourished by fear, superstition, and prejudice.

The period following World War II was characterized by a strong international impetus on mental hygiene, and by a fight against discrimination and intolerance toward other human beings who are "different" on account of their religion, the color of their skin, or their physical disability. Another outgrowth of the second World War was widespread acceptance of the concept of human rehabilitation, even in cases of most severe disablement.

It was against this background that there occurred that remarkable phenomenon in the history of human welfare, the spontaneous emergence in widely separated parts of the world of what has come to be known simply as "the parents' movement" — a revolution (and in some cases one might well say a rebellion) of parents of mentally retarded children, who rose up to fight to gain for their children a measure of the new social justice, the new benefits of rehabilitation and also of the new scientific endeavors. Obviously, a major task facing those parents to gain even public tolerance, let alone public support for their efforts, was to bring about a change in the image of the mentally retarded, and thus to counteract the picture of retarded persons as criminals, as sexual degenerates, as incompetents whose inability to work made them a life-long burden on society.

This new movement stressed a different picture—the child who never grew, the Holy Innocent, the eternal child. The appeal made was obviously to the public's pity—typical of those days was the poster of a retarded child looking out from a barred window, or from behind a fence. One spoke of the forgotten children—"scorn not their simplicity" was another slogan of the appeal to the public in those days. The emphasis was on young retarded children and on their helplessness, with the implication that they had to be the *objects* of compassion and protection all through their lives, since after all they were "eternal children."

The protection they were afforded in those days was protection through specialized care; indeed, the implication often was that the retarded child had to be protected from other children. The specialized programs thus pleaded for were often programs of segregation—benevolent segregation to be sure, but none the less segregation. It is important to recall here that this approach resulted in much attention being focused on the problem of the parents, and this was very much reflected in the professional literature, where we had many books and articles which dwelt at much greater length on what could be done to help the parents carry the emotional burden of having a retarded child than on helping retarded children to be less of a burden to their parents.

Things have moved swiftly in the field of mental retardation, and today we can see many evidences of a different and more sophisticated approach to the problem. The tenor of the appeals to the public have changed from a plea for pity to insistent demands that the mentally retarded receive their fair share of the benefits of society. The focus is no longer solely on the young retarded child. Increasingly there are efforts to make the public understand that retarded children grow up to be retarded adults. The slogan "retarded children can be helped" has now an important sequel: "so they may learn to help" — help themselves, help their families, and as adults help society in the way adults help through productive work.

Of course, there continues to be an emphasis on retarded children and their needs, but it is novel, with a noticeably different, more farsighted orientation. We need to help retarded children so they can grow up and function as adults to the best of their ability, however limited. We have learned that some of our past efforts were self defeating from the point of view of rehabilitation. Today we know that to get the public's wholehearted support for education and rehabilitation of the mentally retarded, we must show their potential for life in society and a contribution to society. Only on this basis can we with confidence plan our campaign for public acceptance.

Fortunately, we no longer are limited to expressing hope or making predictions of what mentally retarded individuals might be able to accomplish if given proper training and a chance at work. We now have eloquent testimony from quite a few countries that it is not only the mildly retarded who can be drawn into the productive life of a nation. Steadily, work opportunities are successfully extended to those who formerly were considered ineducable and unemployable. Moreover, as J.W. Wehrmeijer, one of Holland's most experienced rehabilitation experts, has stated, we cannot even estimate how much farther can be extended the work potential and the social adaptability of these more severely retarded, if given adequate training and education, which, he rightly stresses, must begin in the preschool years.

If your objective is to work towards public acceptance of the mentally retarded, it must mean the acceptance of all the mentally retarded, regardless of age and of the degree of their disability. And this, in turn, of course means that in our campaign we must tell the public about all of them. Here then lies the challenge, but also the difficulty, in our campaign to convey to the public a realistic, dynamic, living picture of mental retardation in its broad ramifications as it extends into all life situations, and as it manifests itself from the mildest to the severest degrees.

Our goal must be public acceptance of the mentally retarded child and the mentally retarded adult, in the schools and on the playgrounds, in the factory, in church, and in all areas of the life of the community where they are able to function.

The acceptance of the mildly retarded adult to employment in appropriate positions of governmental services (recently accomplished in the United States as a direct result of President Kennedy's concern with the problem of mental retardation) is as important in that regard as the decision to admit the most severely retarded young children to medical treatment in general community hospitals. In other words, this new orientation will by no means benefit just those retarded persons who, with our new methods of training, can be helped to secure a regular job or merely employment in a sheltered workshop; even the most profoundly retarded will profit from this more positive approach, which extends to him or her the benefit and dignity of being a person.

What specific ways must be pursued to achieve such increasing acceptance of the mentally retarded? A review of developments in most recent years in countries as different as India and Italy, Canada and Japan, Brazil and Israel, shows that basically there is a striking similarity in the methods which have been and are being successfully used in the fight on behalf of the mentally retarded.

There are first of all the mass media, directed at an unspecified audience, the general public. Newspapers, journals, radio, and television rank, of course, first, as they do in any kind of public information effort. In recent years, excellent movies have become available and their distribution has been greatly furthered through the film loan services of the United Nations. (How many films on mental retardation will be available through these United Nations channels depends largely on how much demand is made for them, and this, of course, depends largely on the interest we can create through our work with public and private organizations in our respective countries.) In many countries, excellent posters have been created and very widely distributed, to call attention to the problem of the mentally retarded; one of the most striking and most beautiful is a painting by one of Finland's leading artists of his own teenage, severely retarded son.

In many countries, there has been instituted a special Day or Week devoted to focusing public attention on the problem of mental retardation. It is most remarkable indeed that in India, beset by so many urgent questions in meeting the most basic needs of its general population, a "National Day" devoted to the mentally handicapped was given much publicity in many of the larger cities. Public demonstrations on the streets are no longer so frequently undertaken in these days of television, yet two years ago in Rome a "Silent March" of parents and friends of the mentally retarded made a deep impression on the public and on the legislature then in session.

Good books on the subject of mental retardation are available in ever increasing number, and many of those suitable for wide public circulation have been translated into various languages. Distinct advances in public information can be achieved by making sure that public libraries not only *have* these books on their shelves, but that the librarians are aware of their significance and the ways in which they can best be utilized.

Excellent pamphlets and low-cost leaflets are also available in many languages. Unfortunately, one often finds that useful material giving general information about mental retardation, published in one country, in the Spanish language for instance, is quite unknown in other Spanish-speaking countries where they would be of immediate usefulness. Here undoubtedly is where the work of the International League of Societies for the Mentally Handicapped can establish better communications between countries and better utilization of existing materials.

While increasingly all these mass media are trying to bring to the public a better knowledge and understanding of the mentally retarded as individuals (as contrasted with mental retardation as a problem), nothing can replace the effectiveness of bringing the mentally retarded under favorable circumstances into the physical presence of the general public. Fear of the unknown is always particularly strong, and one of the first and most effective steps in combating the long-standing fear of the general public towards the mentally retarded is to provide a chance to see them, observe them, and get to know them. (We must be aware that this fear, of course, is not just a fear of some imagined immediate physical danger, but also a vague, projected fear that the fate that has befallen the mentally retarded somehow can affect others.)

Therefore, an important part of any public information campaign should be directed not only to providing adequate information, but also to making the retarded visible in the community. This means, for instance, "open house"—certain days when the general public is invited to observe educational programs for the retarded, vocational training, or a sheltered workshop. Visits of retarded school children to neighborhood stores, fire stations, bus or railroad terminals, are not just important because of the educational value for the children, but frequently this will be the first time that other people actually see a child with mongolism, for instance, participating in a normal activity. But travel around the neighborhood or the city is only part of the picture. For years, the headmaster of a special school in England has taken a large group of his boys on an annual trip to Paris, because trips are common for the regular schools in London, and one of his objectives was to demonstrate to the public that his retarded adolescent boys, too, were capable of conducting themselves well on such an occasion.

Similar trips abroad have been arranged for retarded youngsters in other countries as well, in some cases even by institutions, as is done in Denmark.

Institutions, also, can hold "open house days," inviting members of the general public, first as visitors and later as volunteer helpers. In countries where this is done it has proved a very important bridge to the community for many formerly isolated institutions, resulting in better public knowledge about the institution itself, but also a better and more accepting attitude toward the retarded children and adults in the institution.

While the enlistment of volunteers (who assist primarily with free time activities) will necessarily directly involve only small numbers of the public, it can also be very important in indirect ways. This system of volunteering is especially widespread on the North American continent, but its effective use can be observed in many other countries.

Also to be mentioned in this connection as a frequently used means of bringing the retarded to the attention of the general public are exhibits of their work. This can be particularly effective if the exhibit is sponsored by and in the building of a prestige organization, as, for instance, is done by the savings banks in Spain.

Modern advertising and public relations methods have put much emphasis on the role of the "opinion makers" in present day society. Whether it is in the introduction of new products or in political life, the role of "opinion makers" has received increasing study. Because mental retardation as a life-time disability involves such a wide variety of people and professions, the number of "opinion makers" in this field is very large, but we have too often neglected to make enough use of them in our work. For instance, important as it is to improve the special training provided for teachers in special schools for the retarded, far too long we have failed to concern ourselves with what the average teacher in the ordinary school learns about the problem of mental retardation. Psychiatrists and psychologists are certainly opinion makers in molding the public's attitude towards the mentally retarded, yet what one finds in general psychiatric and psychological textbooks published in the 1960s reflects far too much outdated knowledge of the 1940s. Improving the quality of textbooks is not an easy task, yet nothing will happen unless those working in the field of mental retardation first make it their business to acquaint themselves with these textbooks. It should be stressed here that policies of segregating the mentally retarded by arranging for their medical care, for their education, and for their recreation in separate facilities are particularly disadvantageous from this point of view of the training of professional personnel. Because of this segregation, physicians may go through their training without ever seeing a retarded child, and teachers for normal schools may never meet such children other than in the pages of a textbook.

Thus it should be our urgent concern that all physicians, all psychologists, and all teachers have a knowledge and understanding of the problem of retardation, which leads them to encourage acceptance of the mentally retarded rather than to block it. In some countries, for example, good progress is being made by including helpful, up-to-date information about the mentally retarded and their need for social integration in the curriculum of the secondary schools. Indeed, this may influence some of these young people to choose our field for their future professional training; in any case, it can help to give them a more positive attitude toward the mentally retarded.

Certainly among the important "opinion makers" we must mention in this connection the author Pearl Buck, who was the first person of international renown to make it public knowledge that she had a retarded child. Her example has been followed by outstanding persons in many countries, and each time this happens, we move one step closer to public acceptance.

Another important avenue in the work towards public acceptance of the retarded is opened if prestige organizations can be interested in this cause. In those countries where the Scouts have actively included the mentally retarded in their programs, along with other handicapped youngsters (for instance, Sweden), general support of other recreational activities and indeed on all types of other services for the retarded has increased. When the American Red Cross published, jointly with the National Association for

Retarded Children, a manual on swimming for the retarded, the managers of many swimming pools no longer refused to admit mentally retarded persons to their facilities. Another example of the value of Red Cross support took place here in France when last year the French Red Cross devoted an entire issue of its journal to seven informative articles on mental retardation. For many years the Norwegian Red Cross has played a leading role in providing services for the retarded.

In the development of employment opportunities for the retarded, it is important to have the active support and endorsement of some large, prestigious industrial or commercial companies. The fact that the Philips company in the Netherlands, for example, has been willing to give many contracts to sheltered workshops for the retarded has influenced other employers to do likewise.

For the past three years, the National Association for Retarded Children in the USA has awarded a citation of honor to the "Employer of the Year," in recognition of successful integration of mentally retarded adults into the labor force of a business or industrial enterprise. The presentation is made by an outstanding public official, and the resulting nationwide newspaper publicity stimulates other employers to consider opportunities for employing the retarded.

In the early days of the new movement on behalf of the mentally retarded, the public information campaign fell largely to the association of parents and friends. It is a tribute to the effectiveness of their efforts that today they no longer have to carry this task alone. Progressive public and private organizations in the field of health, welfare, and rehabilitation that offer services to the mentally retarded now realize that they, too, must promote the acceptance of the retarded by the public, if their work is to be successful. As the public schools include more and more programs for the mentally retarded, they also are of necessity working towards public acceptance of the young people whom they have trained. Finally, those organizations which formerly limited their efforts to furthering the rehabilitation of the physically handicapped are slowly but steadily coming to recognize that their concern needs to extend at last in a general way to the mentally handicapped and their acceptance by the public.

The action program that has been indicated in this paper, involving newspapers, journals, radio, television, public events of all types, involvement of business and industry, of leading public figures, and public and private organizations of many types, might easily convey the impression of a task that has far outgrown the voluntary effort of a modest local association in a small town. This is quite in error. Such a small town would undoubtedly have at least a weekly newspaper. The obvious first task would be to find out what kind of news is of interest to the editors and then to provide it. Every small town has its own "opinion makers" whose interest and cooperation must be enlisted. Every small town has its own religious, political, business, or social groups, and the question is only to determine through what particular aspect of the problems of the retarded their interest can be enlisted. Every small town has from time to time a vacant store, and most landlords are willing to permit (in such a situation) the store window to be used for a public information exhibit on mental retardation. Either in the town itself or in the next larger city there will be a library whose cooperation can be gained.

The important point, of course, is that today the Society for the Mentally Handicapped in the small town can depend in its public information effort on assistance from national and international associations. It is true that public acceptance of the mentally retarded can most effectively be promoted on a wide, national scale, yet it is in the local community that the effectiveness of such promotion is put to the test, and no local Community can afford to leave this effort to be carried out by the national organization alone.

Whether our public information effort is in a small or in a metropolitan area, on a local, national, or international level, experience has provided some cautions that need to be observed. The first and most important caution is that the effectiveness of our efforts will depend on the adequacy of the information offered. We must avoid exaggerated and overstated claims, for example, concerning the achievement potential of the retarded; we must avoid superficial and misleading publicity of research findings. Damaging in the long run will be any odious comparisons with other types of handicap. To the contrary, our efforts should always imply the need for public acceptance of all handicapped persons. We must learn when to align our cause with that of other handicapping conditions, although this by no means implies that we should not clearly establish the identity of mental retardation.

And finally our success will depend in part on our sympathetic understanding of and sympathetic reply to the fears of those who speak out against a social integration of the retarded, such as a businessman's fears of unfair competition, labor unions' fears of cheap labor, or the fear expressed in a neighborhood of the danger that would follow the establishment of a hostel for young adult retarded persons.

In the current issue of the British journal *Mental Health*, Bryan Magee has this to say:

> Anything that diminishes ignorance and widens the area of what is publicly acknowledged, diminishes intolerance. And impartial reporting does more to change attitudes than argument can ever do.... This important fact is not yet generally recognized ... so what is most needed for the next push towards a more tolerant society is not more liberal propaganda, but more information.

This clearly indicates the task that is facing all of us in achieving public acceptance of the mentally retarded, locally, nationally, and internationally.

PART VIII

Religious Concerns

Chapter 15
Parish Awareness*

In October 1978, the Seventh World Congress of the International League of Societies for the Mentally Handicapped, meeting in Vienna, attracted participants from no less than 62 countries around the world. Among those who made presentations were a Catholic priest from French Canada, an American Lutheran from the Missouri Synod, and a Moslem director of Islamic cultural affairs in Tunisia.

What is significant is that all three emphasized in essence the same basic message, the need to respect mentally retarded persons as persons, and the need for the religious community, the parish, not only to accept but to seek and facilitate their participation.

This is indeed a far cry from what was expressed earlier in our century. At that time one could hardly say that the Age of Enlightenment had yet set in as far as mental retardation, then known as feeblemindedness and idiocy, was concerned. There was still widespread confusion even among well educated people between mental retardation and mental illness, and this meant that the old demonological beliefs—namely, that such individuals were possessed by the Devil—were still in existence.

I am purposely reminding you of these facts at the beginning of my comments because my general presentation will reflect my own strong optimism, and my faith in the contribution retarded people can and do make. But it is necessary for us to be mindful of the past, as it still reaches into the present and creates among our fellows and in our parishes a resistance which may be hidden, or may be very aggressive and outspoken, but with which we must

---

* *Conference of the National Apostolate with Mentally Retarded Persons, Chicopee, Massachusetts, 1973.*

reckon as we push forward with new and progressive planning and action.

If I were to select the most significant trend in this new and progressive planning in mental retardation, not only in our country but also abroad, I would point to what has become known as the normalization principle.

There is still much confusion and even resentment regarding this term. It should by no means ever be interpreted as an effort to "normalize" mentally retarded individuals. Rather, as it was first formulated in Scandinavia, it reflected the realization that "a specific strategy had to be developed to counteract the process of denormalization which over the past 75 years made such deep inroads into society's stance, society's dealing with handicapped individuals such as persons with epilepsy, mental retardation, cerebral palsy, and a host of other disabilities, and in particular persons with multiple disabilities. In other words, normalization is a rational attempt to deal with the very conditions which have tended to deepen and reinforce prejudice and to set the severely handicapped apart from the rest of society."

The normalization principle, as expressed by Bengt Nirje, means "making available to the mentally retarded . . . patterns and conditions of everyday life which are as close as possible to the norms and patterns of the mainstream of society."

From the normalization principle flow two significant subsidiary ideas: the emphasis on integration of, as the educators phrase it, mainstreaming, and the emphasis on the rights of individuals with mental retardation.

I am happy to say that the Pastoral Statement on Handicapped People, formulated by the U.S. Catholic Bishops at their Conference in November 1978, is in no way in conflict with these broad principles. Indeed, the principle of integration with the affirmation of the rights of all persons with handicaps is expressed in this Statement very directly and clearly.

But significant as has been the progress in the churches' educational work with children, it does not suffice to meet the challenge of your own conference topic today; Parish Awareness: Reaching Out—Receiving. What stands between this challenge and the situations in many if not most parishes has been the church's reluctance to accept the adult person who is mentally retarded into participating membership on a day-to-day basis.

Fr. David Wilson, director of the pastoral office for the handicapped of St. Joseph's Centre, North London, speaks to this problem directly and forcefully: "We have to get rid of the idea that mentally handicapped people are the 'Holy Innocents,' or 'Eternal Children,' or 'Heavenly Peter Pans.' They are people with particular gifts like anyone else."

This change will not be an easy task, particularly because for many parents it has been a source of reassurance for themselves to look upon their mentally retarded young adults as children, to dress them as if they were still children, and to deny them the sense of sexuality which commonly is seen as an important part of growing into adulthood. After all, Pearl Buck entitled the story of her retarded daughter's life "The Child Who Never Grew," and a major production of the Canadian Film Board was called "Eternal Children."

Fortunately, beginning ten to fifteen years ago, there has been a steady turning away from this view. On the international scene, more and more of the voluntary associations have dropped the word children from their names. In our country it was in 1973 that NARC changed its name to National Association for Retarded Citizens. I am happy to tell you that it was at a conference on the social, vocational, and religious integration of mentally retarded persons, arranged in Rome in 1965 by the International Catholic Child Bureau's special commission, that the place of the retarded adult in society was very clearly enunciated.

The keynote speaker, Professor Van Niele of the Netherlands, had this to say:

> We think and talk about the problems in mental retardation, but as we do it, the person with mental retardation cannot take part. Thereby we become one-sided, and this leads to the danger that the retarded person is not being integrated into society, that he must stand outside. The retarded person, however, is part of society, is part of humanity. He is God's creature and part of His plan.

My husband and I participated in this conference and were privileged to be present at an Audience in the Vatican when His Holiness Pope Paul VI strongly echoed these sentiments and emphasized the human community's duty to include handicapped persons in our social, vocational, and religious life. The conclusions of this important international gathering introduced a new concept, the right of the mentally retarded person to participation in society, "a right which is based on natural law."

Two years later, the International League of Societies for the Mentally Handicapped called together in Stockholm a symposium concerning the basic legal and legislative aspects of mental retardation. The conclusions of that symposium contained a brief section on the individual rights of a retarded person. This was of such significance that in the following year, at its 1968 World Congress in Jerusalem, the League's Assembly voted to adopt and promulgate it under the title "Declaration of General and Special Rights of the Mentally Retarded."

Your program committee asked me to include in my presentation some comments on voluntary organizations and their role in this field, and I can think of no better example than this Declaration of Rights to show how voluntary associations can influence or even fashion national or international policy. In most countries, parent associations started modestly as self help groups. Since their retarded children were denied services from all relevant services in the community, parents themselves had to undertake to create some of these services. They soon were able to enlist the aid of professional people and began to plead for help from the local and state authorities. Slowly, there came the awareness that their children were unjustly denied assistance and services to which they should be entitled, and thus the 1968 Jerusalem Congress had the significant and deliberately provocative title, "From Charity to Rights." But not even the most optimistic among the League's leadership would have dared to predict that only three years later this same Declaration would be adopted by the General Assembly of the United Nations.

I cannot refrain from calling to your attention a linguistic detail which really pinpoints what this is all about. The original Declaration put forth by the International League spoke in its title of "the mentally retarded." But the United Nations title changed this to "mentally retarded persons." I am of course very pleased that your organization has also decided to include the word person in its title. It seems urgent that we use this word person as often as possible; all too often, even today, one still hears professional workers and others speak of "retardates" as if they were non-human and a race apart from the rest of humanity.

What is it then that we can do in our parishes to "reach out, to receive?" Once again let me quote from Father Wilson in London:

> If we wish to send people to Lourdes, which for many can be a deeply rewarding experience, then we must ensure that they are not left alone and unwanted on their return. The treatment they receive in Lourdes should be the treatment they receive at home in their own parishes.

But even that is not enough. Jean Vanier, so well known to you as the founder of the L'Arche movement and a true spiritual leader, has given us another challenge:

> If handicapped people are there only to be helped and can bring nothing to others, then they are condemned to a life of simply receiving, of being the last, the most inferior. This will necessarily bring them to depression and a lack of confidence in themselves. This in turn will push them into anguish and make them aggressive towards themselves and others. For them to find real meaning in life, they must find people who sense their utility, their capacity for growth and their place in the community and in the world.

How does the parish go about this task, meet this challenge? Obviously, there are many ways, and as my husband and I traveled in some of the European countries earlier this summer I was on the lookout for material to bring back to you. In fact, it was on the very last day when I found exactly that: a kit of materials prepared by the Diaconate Services of the German Evangelical Church to help parishes in "Living Together with the Handicapped." This first booklet is subtitled "The Situation of the Mentally Retarded: Tasks for the Christian Community," and has detailed suggestions and alternatives for practical action for the parish members. The second is a very well prepared and attractively illustrated book on "What is Mental Retardation" and what can and is being done. Finally, a small flier with cartoon illustrations of some two dozen "TIPS" on things that handicapped and non-handicapped children, adolescents, and adults can do together.

As you know well, very often programs for handicapped persons in the parish are carried on by a few people whose work may not even be known by most of the rest of the congregation. In contrast, this proposal begins with a rather detailed, step-by-step plan of actively involving parishioners themselves in discussion of the issues. But what are the issues? Who really knows how many people with severe handicap, physical or mental, are there in the parish? Where and how are they housed? What are they doing?

An article in a recent Catholic journal published by the association of workers responsible for mental retardation services within the German Caritas organization points up something I would have hesitated to say on my own quite so bluntly. On the basis on an inquiry in his diocese, the writer found that few priests actually knew who were the handicapped people in their parish, largely because they did not appear in church, and in general the families either deliberately concealed the presence of such a family member or else made no effort to involve the priest.

It was with this kind of situation in mind, undoubtedly, that the Evangelical Taskgroup suggested that the first step for a parish to undertake be a fact-finding effort, and be carried out by visiting teams of parishioners (perhaps these are regular parish visitors) who will make an effort to locate persons with severe handicaps, so they can be visited and information gathered about the problem and the specific needs as the family sees them.

Once this effort is completed and the findings evaluated, the next step would be a meeting of parishioners. The first point on the suggested agenda, however, would not be a report of the fact-finding committee, as one would normally expect, but rather an attempt to deal with the very problem that causes handicapped people to be hidden and to remain isolated—namely, the discomfort of non-handicapped people in the presence of those with severe handicap. It is this point which is somewhat difficult to relate in a brief presentation, but which in a very real and vital way makes such a meeting different from the kind of "public information" sessions about handicap that I know many churches have carried out.

But there is one other point in the German proposal which is both consequential and basic. It is that, right from the beginning, handicapped persons themselves and not only their families will be invited and helped to participate in these parish meetings. At first, it may be difficult to find mentally handicapped individuals who are ready to take part, but they are there; one of the most encouraging developments I have been privileged to observe in England, Sweden, Canada, and in our own country, from Oregon to Massachusetts, has been the way in which retarded young and not so young adults are learning to express their own feelings and ideas, and their own perception of being like other people, or to use the name of their own organizations, to be "People First," even though handicapped.

What I want to emphasize here is that it is of rather limited value merely to give people information about the problem of handicap. Inevitably, the program committee looks around for an expert who will come with a learned lecture on the causes of mental retardation, its incidence and prevalence, information about available programs, the goals of comprehensive planning. None of this touches the key problem, our need to understand our own personal, often perhaps hidden feelings about handicap, and, conversely, the feelings and conceptions of the handicapped people themselves. Inevitably, this will confront the participant in such a meeting with another point which surely will bring controversy, perhaps even among this audience—namely, the excessive valuation placed in our society on intelligence, and the excessive devaluation of persons whose intelligence is limited.

It is essential for the parishioners to learn and to experience that, while their retarded friends may be slow in their thinking in their day-to-day life, their friends' capacity to feel and to express their feelings is a gift they can make to our society.

The German booklet suggests that some role-playing might be

helpful in such a meeting in an effort to make this message more realistic. Even some skillfully presented vignettes describing the life patterns of a person with mental retardation can be of great help in bringing about a better understanding, and such a story of a young man is included (with accompanying slides available). My husband and I like to tell the story of a young woman with Down's syndrome we know in Warsaw, Poland. She had some schooling and can read a little, but she knows a lot about house-keeping, can do simple shopping, and does some cooking. In her free afternoons she goes to a nearby School for Blind Children where she helps in the recreation programs. When her parents return from work in the early evening, they come to a clean and tidy house, and the supper table is laid.

On our and most nations' public scale of value, she would rank at the bottom, considered unemployable or, as our Rehab people say, "not feasible for employment," and in the health statistics she would be carried as "chronically disabled." Yet she actually does contribute to the GNP — the gross national product, by enabling both parents to work. She provides needed emotional support for her elderly parents, and if the community would look and listen, they would appreciate her as a person with warmth for reaching out to others with handicaps, as a diligent person who indeed is making a contribution to the common good.

But what happens when her parents die? If only the commu-nity — and that of course in our context means first of all her parish — would accept her as a valuable person, a contributing member, instead of denigrating her, in statistics as well as in fact, as a liability. It would not be hard to work out a social situation where she would continue to live and contribute, in her own modest way, to the wellbeing of others. She is not "a mongoloid," a term I detest and am sorry to encounter still in the writings and statements of people in our field. She is a person with Down's syndrome, just as much as her priest may be a person with heart disease and not "a cardiac."

But merely to hear about someone like our young Polish friend, or even to see her in her daily activities on a video tape, is not going to be enough. Nobody expects one parish meeting, no matter how carefully planned, to bring about meaningful, lasting change. And so the German parish program lays out a long term follow-up plan with a variety of suggested activities which would involve enough members of the congregation to make a difference in the long run. It is suggested, for instance, that out of such a meeting could develop a number of action committees to follow up on particular problems reported by the visiting teams regarding the life of persons with severe handicap in the parish, perhaps relating to transportation, housing, health needs. Another suggestion is to develop a way for some handicapped and non-handicapped adults to meet together on a continuing basis around some activity, perhaps something that would benefit the parish. There is much room for club activity—not clubs for handicapped parishioners, but parish clubs which will welcome in their midst some handicapped persons.

There is not time to refer here to all the planning details in the German program, but their direction is very clear—to include persons with handicap fully in the activities of the parish. There are dangers of course, and one is that an overdose in enthusiasm will result in too much one-sided activism.

In a British Catholic journal, Fr. McCollagh of Northern Ireland echoes Jean Vanier's reminder to us that "we are too much concerned with what we can do for handicapped persons, and not enough for what we can help them to do for others."

In Birmingham, England, a young friend of ours translated this fine philosophy into practice a few years ago. He recruited some volunteers from his high school and organized a one-to-one get-acquainted program with one of the larger community homes or hostels serving retarded men. After good contacts had been established, a proposal was made that they go out in the community and assist aged people who had special needs. This sounded fine to the hostel residents, and so, in teams of two, they visited elderly people, helped them with chores, painted some kitchens, fixed some leaking faucets, weeded some little garden patches, helped some people just get out for walks. Some of the men from the hostel were middle aged, yet it was the first time they had ever been able to be of assistance to other people, the first time they had the feeling of being needed.

It is important to remember that for the adult person with mental retardation the parish church should not only be an important place for worship and for socialization (usually something arranged for them), but also a place for love, friendship, and genuine acceptance as the adults they are.

In the life of the church there is much emphasis on "witness." To me, not only the most exciting but also the most promising development in the field of mental retardation is the "witnessing" we now hear on the part of retarded people themselves. It is not always spoken clearly, so we must listen carefully. Perhaps "talk less and listen more" might be a good exhortation for all of us who work with retarded persons. And, as we listen, with an open mind, we will continue to discover that much of our work of the past was based on the wrong premises. One factor stands out in particular—an almost universal underestimation of the human potential of these persons.

Without in any way criticizing the educational programs of the past, what we are now learning from our retarded adult friends certainly requires a searching reappraisal of our educational goals and aspirations for retarded children. Thus, all of us, workers, parents, and friends, can look toward the future, confident of the progress that will be made.

References

Bank-Mikkelsen, N.E. 1980. Denmark. In *Normalization, social integration and community*, ed. R.J. Flynn and K.E. Nitsch. Baltimore: University Park Press.

Brimblecombe, F. 1978. Early partnership. In *Congress Proceedings, 7th world congress of ILSMH*. Brussels: The International League of Societies for the Mentally Handicapped.

Byrne, A. 1971. The health visitor and the family with a retarded child. In *The team approach*. London: National Society for Mentally Handicapped Children.

Carter, D. 1976. The advisory service for rural training, employment occupations and settlement of the mentally handicapped. Reprint. London: Kings Fund Center (KFC/76/180).

Center on Human Policy. 1979. The community imperative: A refutation of all arguments in support of institutionalizing anybody because of mental retardation.. Syracuse: The Center on Human Policy.

Chapplett, E., and G. Morier. 1968. Declaration of the rights of the child: A historical review. *International Child Welfare Review* 22: 4-8.

Dawson, S. 1988. Personal communication with author.

Department of Health and Social Services. 1972. *Better services for the mentally handicapped*. London: HMSO.

Fletcher, J. 1972. Indicators of humanhood—A tentative profile of man. *Hastings Center Report* 5:1.

Forrel, A., and M. Gluc. 1979. Noah's ark toy library for handicapped children. *Australia Journal of Mental Retardation* 5: 325-326.

Holt, K. 1974. Medical and developmental issues. In *Proceedings of 1st annual congress, Association of Professions for the Mentally Handicapped*. London: The Association of Professions for the Mentally Handicapped.

ILSMH. 1979. Comments prepared by P. Mittler and Mme. Y. Posternak.

International Labor Organization. 1955. *Recommendation 99.* Geneva: International Labor Organization.

International League of Societies for the Mentally Handicapped. 1967a. *Symposium on sheltered employment.* Frankfurt, 1966. International League of Societies for the Mentally Handicapped.

International League of Societies for the Mentally Handicapped. 1967b. *Legislative aspects of mental retardation—Conclusions.* Stockholm Symposium. Stockholm: International League of Societies for the Mentally Handicapped.

International League of Societies for the Mentally Handicapped. 1968. *From charity to rights.* 4th International Congress, Jerusalem 1968. Brussels: International League of Societies for the Mentally Handicapped.

International League of Societies for the Mentally Handicapped. 1971. *Report on the International Symposium on cooperation between parents, clients, and staff.* Brussels: The International League of Societies for the Mentally Handicapped.

International League of Societies for the Mentally Handicapped. 1978b. *Step by step: Guidelines on implementation of the declaration on the rights of mentally retarded persons.* Brussels: The International League of Societies for the Mentally Handicapped.

Jaffe, M., and T. Smith. 1986. *Siting group homes for developmentally disabled persons.* Chicago: American Planning Association.

Jones, A. 1975. Assessment: A means to an end? *New Psychiatry* 2:8.

Miles, M. 1980. A school on the north west frontier: Special education/Forward trends. *British Journal of Special Education* 7(2): 33.

Nirje, B. 1969. Toward independence. Paper presented at the 11th World Congress of the International Society for the Rehabilitation of the Disabled, Dublin. Mimeo.

Partlow Review Committee. 1978. In Motion for modification. Wyatt v. Hardin (Civil Action No. 3195N, 20 October). Middle District, Alabama.

Portray, R. 1988. Personal communication with author.

Posternak, Y. 1979. *The integration of handicapped children and adolescents in Italy.* Paris: Centre for Educational Research and Innovation.

Segal, S. 1967. No child is ineducable. London: Pergamon.

Semiawan, C. 1980. Applying integration when resources are limited. Paper read at the World Congress on Rehabilitation, Winnipeg.

Shearer, A. 1978. Meeting vocational and social needs. In *Proceedings, 7th world congress of the ILSMH*. Brussels: The International League of Societies for the Mentally Handicapped.

Shearer, A. 1985. *Looking forward: Report on an ILSMH symposium on the future of voluntary associations*. Brussels: The International League of Societies for Persons with Mental Handicap.

Spain, G., and C. Wigley. 1975. *Right from the start—A service for families with a young handicapped child*. London: National Society for Mentally Handicapped Children.

Spudich, H. 1988. Personal communication with author.

Tizard, B. 1975. Beyond the nursery. *Times Educational Supplement*, 25 April.

Tizard, J. 1965. Personal communication with the author.

UNESCO. 1971. *A study of the present situation of special education*. Paris.

UNESCO. 1979a. *Final report, expert meeting on special education*. ED-79/Conf. 606/21.

UNESCO. 1979b. *Report of the regional seminar on the education of mentally retarded children*. Paris.

United Nations. 1948. *Universal declaration of human rights*. New York: United Nations.

United Nations. 1971. *Declaration on the rights of mentally retarded persons*. New York: United Nations.

Vanier, J. 1974. *The contribution of the physically and mentally handicapped to development*. Paper presented at the International Conference on Social Welfare, 16 July, in Nairobi, Kenya. Mimeo.

Winterbourn, R. 1965. Formation au foyer par correspondence—Une experience Neo-Zelandaise. *Revue Internationale de l'Enfant*, 24:4.

Biographical Note

Rosemary Ferguson Dybwad was born May 12, 1910 in Howe, Indiana, and spent her childhood in that midwestern state. Because her father became minister of the Union Church in Manila, she lived as an adolescent in the Philippines, with visits to China and Japan.

As an undergraduate student at Western College for Women, Oxford, Ohio, she met several foreign students. This inspired her to apply to the Institute of International Education for a fellowship at a German university. She was a graduate student in Sociology at the University of Leipzig from 1931-33. In 1935, she returned to Germany to attend the University of Hamburg, receiving her doctorate in 1936.

In 1934, she married Gunnar Dybwad, whom she had met while studying at Leipzig, and during the early years together they both worked in correctional institutions in Indiana, New Jersey and New York. She terminated her employment after the birth of her son in 1939, who was joined by a sister in 1941.

While her husband served as Director of Child Welfare in Michigan, 1943-1951, the Dybwad home welcomed a steady stream of United Nations Fellows and foreign students from around the world. This hospitality to visitors from abroad continued through the ensuing decades.

When her husband became executive director of the National Association for Retarded Children in 1957, Rosemary volunteered to look after an increasing volume of correspondence from foreign countries that reached the Association's headquarters. The ensuing exchange of information led her to initiate an international newsletter which contributed to the eventual establishment of the European, and later, the International League of Societies for Persons with Mental Handicap.

In 1964, she and her husband became co-directors of an international mental retardation project in Geneva which took them as consultants to some 30 countries around the globe. After returning to the USA, colleagues persuaded her to use her global knowledge to edit an international directory of mental retardation resources. First published in 1971, the third edition of this unique source of international information was completed by her in 1989.